Branding & Sales:::The LinkedIn Way

Branding & Sales
The LinkedIn Way

Jasmine Sandier

Branding & Sales:::The LinkedIn Way

Branding & Sales
The LinkedIn Way

First Edition

Copyright 2012
All rights reserved Jasmine Sandler

All rights reserved. No part of this book may be: reproduced in any form or by any electronic or mechanical means, including information storage and retrieval systems, without permission in writing from the publisher, except by a reviewer who may quote brief passages in a review. This book would not have been possible without screenshots from LinkedIn.com.

Dedication

This book is dedicated to my brother, Jonathan Sandler, who passed away in 2009 due to diabetes complications. I will actively support the National Juvenile Diabetes Foundation and its efforts to cure the disease with proceeds from the sales of this book and future books from JS Publishing. I also want to thank my Mom and my fiancée for their continued support.

Contents

Copyright 2012 2
Dedication 2
Preface 5
LinkedIn is the Ultimate Branding & Sales Tool 5
    The Importance of LinkedIn for 6
    Building Your Business 6
    Chapter 1 6
    Investing in LinkedIn Marketing 14
    Creating a Visible & Engaging 20
    LinkedIn Profile 20
    Your LinkedIn Company Page 31
    Using LinkedIn Tools 34
SECTION II 49
LinkedIn Marketing 49
    Your LinkedIn Personal Brand 49
    Content Creation for an Engaging Personal Brand 53
    Getting Found on LinkedIn 58
    The SEO connection 58
    Leveraging LinkedIn across all 63
    your Web Marketing 63
    Advertising On LinkedIn 66
    Your LinkedIn Marketing Plan 68
SECTION III: SALES 69
    Creating & Building Your 69
    LinkedIn Network 69
    LinkedIn Sales Etiquette 72
    LinkedIn Sales Planning and Scoring 75
    Recommendations & Endorsements 80
    Emphasis on Necessary LinkedIn Sales Tools in Premium Accounts 82
    Deciphering LinkedIn Analytics 84

Afterward: LinkedIn Member Services: 85
    Hopeful Changes 85
Thank you 88
Author's Bio...89

Preface
LinkedIn is the Ultimate Branding & Sales Tool

After close to 20 years of Online Marketing and B2B Sales work, I have found myself, as I am sure you can appreciate, interested in spending my limited time on building only qualified business relationships. To me this means those who help grow my brand and market position, drive profitability, provide cost-savings or all of the above. I can confidently say that my efforts in LinkedIn have and continue to provide me with all of these benefits.

I first joined LinkedIn in 2005 and, then, used it lightly as a connection tool, as something to store my rolodex of cards from tradeshows, networking events and client meetings. In the last five (5) years, LinkedIn, as a marketing and sales tool has completely exploded.

Today, LinkedIn represents 175+MM business decision makers in over 200 countries. Because of LinkedIn's ability to drive awareness around an individual as well as deliver targeted, warm inbound leads, it is a personal branding and sales tool on steroids. There are multiple marketing benefits to using LinkedIn, which I will explore throughout this book, including personal and corporate branding, search engine visibility, targeted focus group and direct response opportunities.

LinkedIn should be any Marketing and Sales professional's cornerstone for personal branding online and qualified lead generation. The sales guide that follows has been written for the hundreds of LinkedIn trainees that kept asking me for a "manual" to quickly and easily guide them through using LinkedIn as their #1 Sales and Marketing tool.

This is not meant be yet another LinkedIn "How To Use" book. Of course, I will cover the LinkedIn "use" basics; but this guide has truly been created for the purpose of Branding and Selling through LinkedIn. Additionally, for all my fellow LinkedIn advocates, as a way to ensure a positive ROI from your LinkedIn efforts. Read on, take action and start to see immediate results from effective LinkedIn Marketing. Enjoy.

SECTION 1: LinkedIn Basics

The Importance of LinkedIn for Building Your Business
Chapter 1

LinkedIn is the largest and most active social networking site for business professionals, with over 175 million registered LinkedIn profiles(2012) globally and counting. As the world's premier B2B Social Networking tool, LinkedIn provides an optimal platform for business networking, real-time market research, recruiting/job opportunities and online branding for both individual professionals and companies.

Since the fall of the global economy in 2001 and then again in 2008/9, there has been a dramatic increase in start-up development, competition in general business and a rise in unemployment. Because of these three important factors, it has become crucial for business professionals to become more polished, sharp and well-connected than ever before.

LinkedIn can and should be the primary social media tool for anyone selling business to business. This is why the LinkedIn population has grown from 70 million to 175 million+ in just a few short years (from 2006-2012). There are multiple reasons for its explosive growth and success as the primary personal marketing tool of business professionals:

1. LinkedIn is the ultimate business networking tool.
Unlike traditional business networking, doing so on LinkedIn is unlimited. Further, LinkedIn makes it possible for anyone to make business connections with professionals they might never have, and on a global basis. Once you start really connecting on LinkedIn, you will find that you will have millions of possible business connects of real decision makers in your own network and only up to 2 introductions away (if in your 3rd level network). In my LinkedIn network, as an example, I have 1700+ 1st connects with whom I communicate regularly. Those connects and their connects lead me to over 14MM possible business connections. Now it becomes just a matter of qualifying them as possible clients for my online marketing agency, Agent-cy Online Marketing, Inc.! In all seriousness, the point here is that the opportunities for actionable business networking, meaning driving real qualified leads to your door(or in this case, profile) is unlimited. I will share much more on this topic (effective business networking on LinkedIn) in the later chapter, "LinkedIn Networking for Business Relationship Development."

2. LinkedIn has become a recruiter's #1 web marketing tool. More jobs are being posted on LinkedIn than ever before and that is only expected to rise. More jobs mean more candidates. More candidates mean more LinkedIn users. More of the same means more active Company Profiles.

3. The strong need on the web for executives and business professionals to build their own Personal Brands.
With over-saturation and heavy competition online in major industries, including financial services, insurance, web marketing, I.T. services, travel, health & wellness and real estate, individuals have realized that to sell they need to be visible and engaging. Thus, personal branding online has become an essential and also a crowded space. LinkedIn and its pleasing personal profiling make it an obvious personal

branding tool. I will review how you can develop a strong personal brand in LinkedIn in a later chapter.

LinkedIn Usage

So that you fully understand your sales and marketing opportunities on LinkedIn, I thought it would be helpful to provide you with a current (2012) breakdown of LinkedIn active users. Please note these statistics came directly from LinkedIn:

- 175 Million Business Owners Globally (as of August 2, 2012):
- 40% Small Business Professionals
- 20% C-level executives from mid-large-sized organizations
- 25% High-Tech Managers
- 15% Small Business Owners
- 80m members in the U.S
- 9m+ members in Brazil as of August 2, 2012
- 5m+ members in Canada as of January 19, 2012
- 1m+ members in the UAE as of October 1, 2012
- *39m+ members in Europe as of June 30, 2012*
- 10m+ members in the UK as of September 17, 2012
- 4m+ members in France as of September 5, 2012
- 3m+ members in the Netherlands as of December 6, 2011
- 3m+ members in Spain as of March 27, 2012
- 3m+ members in Italy as of September 18, 2012
- 2m+ members in the DACH region (Germany, Austria and Switzerland)
- 1m+ members in Belgium as of September 22, 2011
- 1m+ members in Sweden as of June 20, 2012
- 1m+ members in Turkey as of February 10, 2012
- *30m+ members in Asia and the Pacific as of June 30, 2012*
- 16m+ members in India as of August 1, 2012
- 3m+ members in Australia as of March 12, 2012
- *4m+ members in Southeast Asia as of January 29, 2012*
- 1m+ members in Indonesia as of February 21, 2012
- 1m+ members in the Philippines as of March 12, 2012

So let's look at what these above stats and information mean to you as a LinkedIn marketer. You may want to consider expanding your marketing reach to global users. To do so, you will need a plan that makes sense to that region's culture and demand for your product or service. If you do decide to market yourself in other areas and countries, a good place to start would be to review local Groups in LinkedIn Groups. Of course, it is not that simple; you will have to show real cause and effort in creating operations in those selected areas.

As a national expansion example, my company, Agent-cy Online Marketing, is headquartered in New York City, but has served clients in the Chicago area since 2008 and is now planning to open full operations in Chicago in 2013. And so, when I request to connect with say, Linked N Chicago (LiNC), the largest business LinkedIn Business Group for Chicago, I introduce myself to the organizer of the Group in the following way:

"Thank you, Mary, for the opportunity to Join LiNC. My name is Jasmine Sandler. I am the CEO of a NYC-based Online Marketing & PR agency, Agent-cy Online Marketing (www.agent-cy.com). We serve clients globally and have served several clients in the Chicago area. As part of my formal expansion of Agent-cy in Chicago in 2013, I am interested in locating professionals with whom to work (as part of the Agent-cy team) in the local area. I welcome all inquiries from the LiNC Group and will be in Chicago on 11/13 speaking at SES on LinkedIn Marketing (http://sesconference.com/chicago/agenda-day1.php) Hope to meet you then. Thank you for your time.

Jasmine Sandler

Regional development is just the beginning; LinkedIn's global marketplace provides rapid expansion and market share opportunities in B2B that were unseen in the days before Social Networking. There are a few ways you can start to build a global expansion plan. You can look at Global LinkedIn Members on Google Earth on http://newin.linkedin.com/ to find new LinkedIn global users:

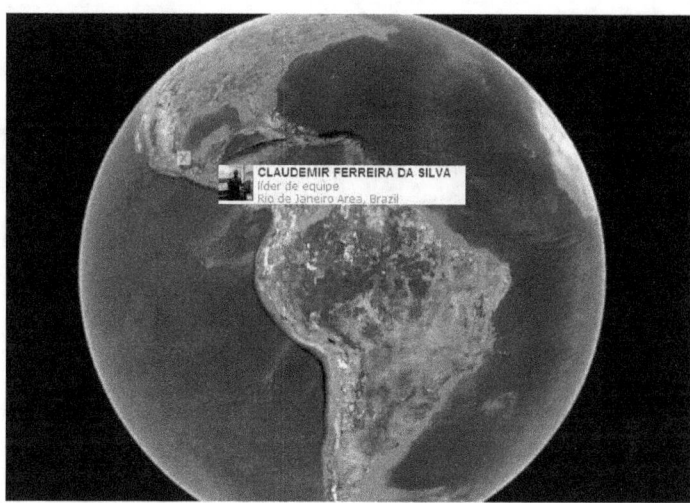

You can get a global map of your connects by utilizing this neat LinkedIn tool, LinkedIn InMaps, which allows you to visualize your network and color code groups that share similarities, such as previous employer or conference attendees, such as those at SES Chicago 2012. To try InMaps, go to http://inmaps.linkedinlabs.com/. In being able to visualize how my subgroups and internal networks were connected and how they then connected to business professionals outside of the U.S., it helped me to build a plan for warm introduction to potential business in Europe and Asia.

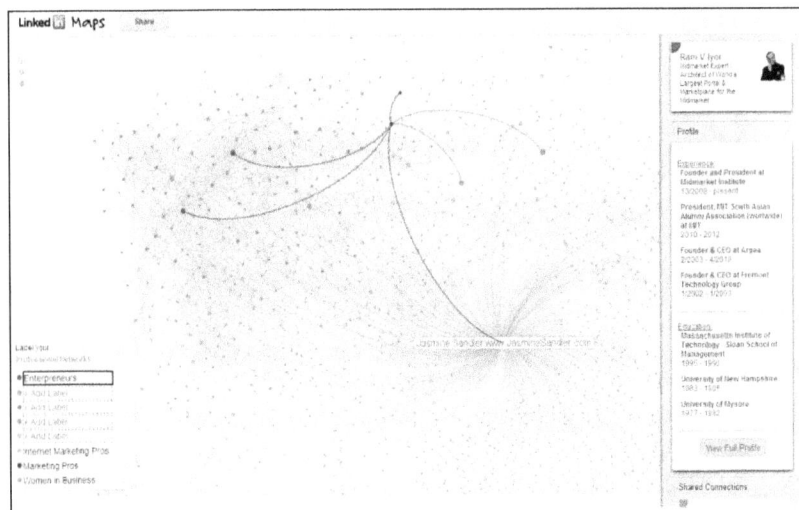

With this tool, you can color code groups by categories. You can then drill down to see associations. From here, you can gain insight not only how people are connected; but also how those groups may serve your individual needs in using LinkedIn as a branding and sales tool. By taking the time to "map" out your connections into groups and locations, you can easily search and locate international business opportunities.

With a Premium account, you can view where your profile page visitors are coming from, what industry they are in and what keywords they used to find you. This information may be helpful to you once you establish your online personal brand on LinkedIn and start proactively to market yourself to people outside of your local area. To access this information, click on Who Has Viewed Your Profile and the number in Blue. You will then see information like this on the right hand side of your screen:

Top Countries	Views
United States	1,259
India	57
Canada	25
United Kingdom	19
Germany	15
World Total	1463

LinkedIn frequency of usage has also exploded, in correlation with the growth of Mobile and Tablets, at 3 Billion Smartphone owners and 1 Billion Tablet owners by 2013(and growing). The LinkedIn app, if you are not familiar, makes it easy to send and respond to messages, update your network with status updates, read the daily news from your network, check daily signals of network updates, engage in Groups and more. The new LinkedIn Mobile Apps have accounted for a 15% increase globally of global new LinkedIn member sign-ups (October 2012).

Some of the latest features include (taken from LinkedIn.com/help)

On iPhone and Android:

1. **Get notified:** LinkedIn keeps you notified in real-time when someone likes what you've shared on LinkedIn, views your profile, accepts your invitation, and much more.

2. **Company pages goes mobile:** Find out which connections work at the companies you care about, see recent news and updates from the company, and learn about current job openings.

3. **Don't want your employer to know you're looking?** LinkedIn recently added access to in which you may be interested directly within your mobile update stream.

On the iPad:

- **6 new languages:** More than 60% of LinkedIn members are based outside the US. LinkedIn now supports French, German, Italian, Spanish, Brazilian Portuguese, and Korean in addition to the other languages already available.

- **Notifications and Company Pages:** Also available on iPad

Investing in LinkedIn Marketing
Chapter 2

You may think … "All of these opportunities to expand my business globally, gain brand awareness and create business relationships on LinkedIn sound great, but what do I need to invest?" The good news is that if you do it right (your LinkedIn presence and marketing efforts) you will be able to realize a positive return on your investment quickly. Using LinkedIn to your advantage requires a solid LinkedIn Marketing Plan and commitment to the plan (management and constant monitoring). That plan needs to be developed with your personal brand and company market position in mind. Some of the crucial items I recommend in which you invest to ensure your success in LinkedIn Marketing are the following:

LinkedIn Education

You are doing this right now. Good work! There are also loads of materials available on my site at www.jasminesandler.com, including webinar and webcast recording, interview recordings, my LinkedIn Marketing whitepaper, LinkedIn training presentations and daily tips on my Blog. Of course, I offer custom individual and corporate training by phone, via webinar and in person. Beyond my materials, you should also stay aware of any and all changes in LinkedIn itself. The tool, its design and functionalities are changing daily. It is in your best interest to stay up to date with the changes happening on LinkedIn. For an insider's look, subscribe to the LinkedIn Blog feed as I do http://blog.linkedin.com/, which provides daily coverage of:

- LinkedIn Extensions
- LinkedIn App partners
- LinkedIn News of the Day
- LinkedIn Marketing Tips
- LinkedIn Functionality Changes
- LinkedIn Profile Design Changes
- LinkedIn Quarterly Reports

Additionally, LinkedIn provides now an expansive Learning Center, where you can get up to date quickly on all the functions and features within LinkedIn at http://learn.linkedin.com/.

There are plenty of LinkedIn trainers out there who talk about how much time you need to spend on LinkedIn. In my experience, if you really want to make LinkedIn your #1 tool for marketing, branding and sales management, you will need to understand how to use the tools (the ones that are and aren't working on LinkedIn), stay aware of the changes to design and functionalities and the opportunities present in Premium member options as well as targeted advertising. I suggest that you do not prescribe a specific time limit to LinkedIn. Would you do that with your current sales and marketing tools, such as Salesforce, Exact Target, SurveyMonkey, etc.? Because, in my humble opinion, LinkedIn can accomplish all (sum of) what these types of tools can do. I encourage you to think of LinkedIn more holistically, as an integral part of your personal branding, company branding and sales active programs.

So, now let's take a look at the investment of upgrading to LinkedIn Premium account, primarily the Sales Premium features. A free account is a good way to start with LinkedIn, but lacks certain aspects essential for sophisticated Sales work. Please note I make NO money from LinkedIn, so anything I discuss around Premium accounts are my opinions based on my direct experience using these tools.

At minimum, you will want to test the **Sales Basic (@ $19.95/month)** account. This allows you to build leads and save lead searches using "Lead Builder". Further, this account gives you advanced Search filters (4) above the free account. This can be very effective as a way to do targeted marketing via geography, title and seniority.

As you build and save your leads, you can track how people in current networks may be directly connected to those with whom you wish to create a business relationship. Whenever I travel to a new city to do business, I prepare a lead list and proactively reach out to those within my network who may be able to make warm introductions for me.

Once you have this account, it is as easy as going into People Search and clicking on Build Lead List. From there, you will be able to choose your filters:

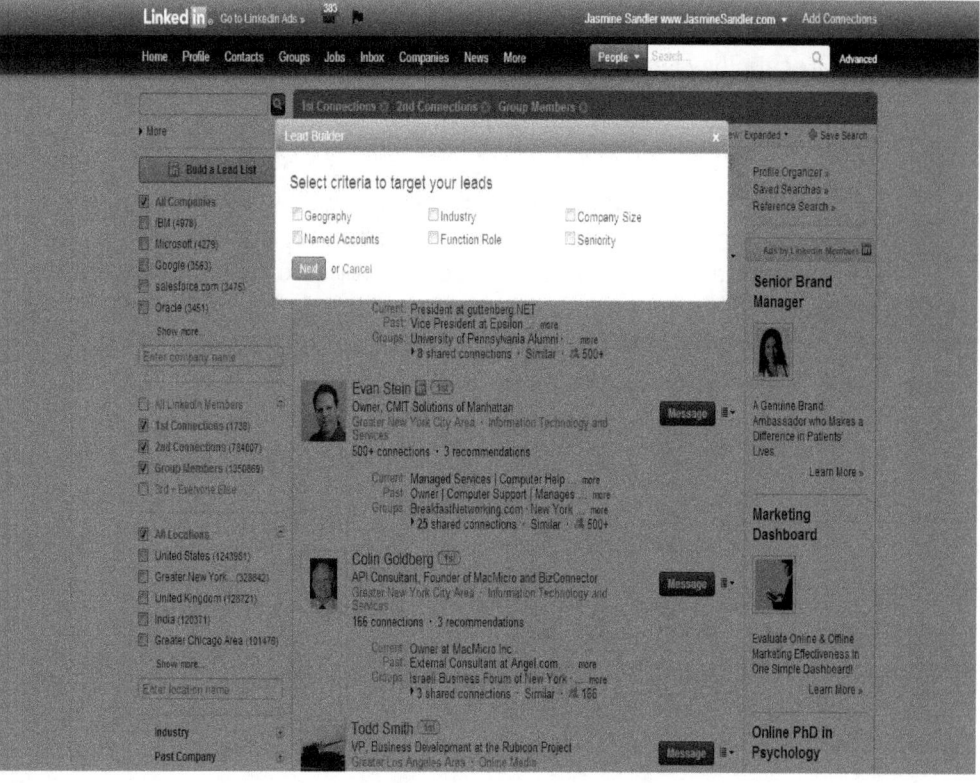

Once you create a Lead List, you can drill down to look at the individual and see shared connections and ways to get a warm introduction. Of course, for this to be effective, you should have a targeted plan for outreach, including why you want to connect with these people and how you can serve them directly based on your case studies and their responsibilities. I will cover Sales Planning more in the Sales section of this book.

In Sales Basic, once you have a saved Lead List as a whole, you can take it a step further to save individual Profiles using Profile Organizer. With Profile Organizer, you can Group Profiles into categories, such as Top Prospects, Hot Leads, Warm Leads and Influencers. As an example, I have created multiple categories based on the types of clients my company, Agent-cy Online Marketing, provides services for. I have done this for the multiple cities we serve, such as:

- Commercial Real Estate Developers
- General Construction Companies
- Architecture and Design Firms
- Technology Services
- Luxury Retail (Can break this down even further into: Fine Jewelry, Apparel, Furniture)

Please note that with the Sales Basic paid account, you can only have up to 5 category folders. As is good Sales practice, you will want to check on and take action within these categories often through the communication sales funnel. You can do this by the ability Profile Organizer provides in adding notes to specific profiles, as you would as a call note in Salesforce, for example.

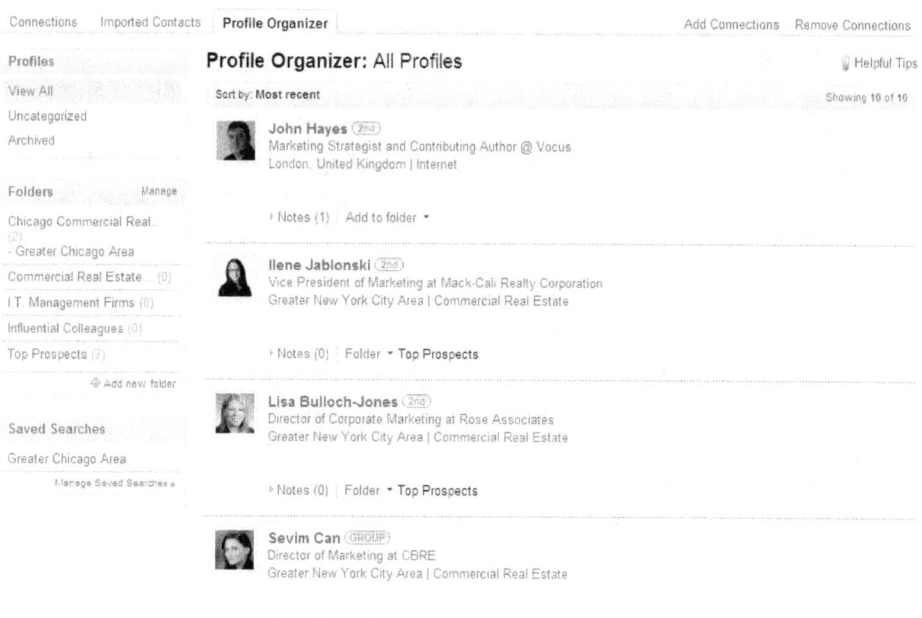

A good tip for making Your Lead Building and Profile Organizing activities to work for you is for you to check the references of the profiles of the people with whom you want to do business. You may find a 1st connect there who can give you real information and a warm introduction. I will cover more on my opinions and specific examples on effective warm introductions in my Sales section of this book.

The last thing worth mentioning with this account type is what LinkedIn calls Priority Customer Service. Unfortunately, I have yet to experience this in my upgraded service. However, with all the nice changes that LinkedIn is introducing with the personal and company profile, etc. we are hoping that LinkedIn will step up its customer service. I will cover more on this in my final opinion on LinkedIn in my last chapter **LinkedIn Member Services – Issues and Hopeful Changes.**

The next tier up under Premium accounts is Sales Navigator @$49.95/Month. Besides giving you more Profile Organizing folders (25), the key upgrade is the opportunity to send anyone in the LinkedIn network a message. This is called an "Inmail". InMails are response guaranteed: if you don't get a response to an InMail within 7 days, LinkedIn will return the credit to your account. Unused InMails rolls over and accumulates for up to 90 days while you are a subscriber. With Sales Navigator, you get up to 10InMails a month.

The highest tier for Marketing & Sales Pros is LinkedIn's **Sales Executive** tier @ **$99/Month.** With Sales Executive, you get up to 25 InMails, 8 Filters on Advanced Search, including In Your Groups which can be very helpful for direct messaging, 50 Folders in Profile Organizer and the ability to see up to 700 Profiles when you search, giving you more opportunities to find your exact target.

If you are a Sales Manager, LinkedIn offers ways for you to see who on your team are connected to possible qualified leads. Team discounts are available as well.

Paying for LinkedIn Premium tools should only support the personal brand and LinkedIn profile you have created. This is the truest way to have a successful marketing and selling experience in LinkedIn. So now let's look at how you can create an engaging Profile.

Creating a Visible & Engaging LinkedIn Profile
Chapter 3

To generate qualified ongoing leads and real business relationships via LinkedIn means that you must have a profile that is visible to LinkedIn search and that is engaging to your target user. To do so, requires both upfront and ongoing work.

In sound marketing efforts for any brand, in this case, a personal brand, a well thought-out strategy precedes execution. Following execution, of course, requires continual monitoring, measurement and content/campaign development. The success of your personal brand depends on your ability to set up and manage your marketing efforts effectively. Let's start on your profile with the first crucial item – your headshot.

1. Your photo

The first essential element to an engaging profile is to show a professional headshot. A headshot must be done by a professional portfolio photographer. A good headshot for LinkedIn can be either a professional headshot with an engaging, appropriate background that suits your line of work or an action shot of you in high-resolution in a business setting, such as you delivering a consult to a client. The file size limit to a LinkedIn photo (today) is 4MB and the scale is that of a thumbnail.

You want to stay away from low-resolution, hard to view or unprofessional imagery. Remember that journalists have free Premium accounts on LinkedIn; for a reason in that they use LinkedIn a source of material for their stories. Journalists, reporters and managing editors are sticklers for their editorial guidelines and a pro headshot in high-resolution is an absolute. For an example of great headshot work, scroll through Jason Gardner's online portfolio in NYC(www.jasongardner.net(or in Chicago, Adam Daniels (http://www.adamdaniels.com) , both of whom are in my network of nation-wide best of the best portfolio photographers for LinkedIn personal brand development.

Since you are reading this book and therefore serious about your image on LinkedIn, note that it is ok for you to have an illustrator do some light re-touching of your photo. I personally recommend Victor Rojas, illustrator, with whom I have worked extensively on client re-touching. You want a photo that truly captures you at your best in your business setting. Your photographer can help you decide what that looks like; but of course, I encourage you to provide that person with direction. It is your photo, after all. With the new LinkedIn Profile Design, you will have the ability to increase your headshot size to double of what it is now:

See my photo as an example. I had this shot by my pro photographer partner here in NYC during a live LinkedIn corporate training session in my offices. I chose the place and occasion. I tend to become very animated when I present and so I wanted Jason to capture that on camera. During the 90 minute corporate LinkedIn training presentation, he must have shot over 100 photos. I then went through those to decide on the one photo that clearly showed me in my true form. This is the result, which is live on my LinkedIn profile today:

I have many other HD photos ready to go the minute that LinkedIn moves me to the new LinkedIn profile (I am in the queue and if you have not yet asked to be moved, please do so at
http://www.linkedin.com/profile/sample)

2. Your profile headline

Your profile headline is as equally important as your headshot so it should be equally supportive (to your personal brand). When creating your headline you want to think of your top three strengths and services which you want to promote and can support. These should be the three things at which you are best, for which you want to be known and where you know you shine. Your headline needs to read the like a direct response ad for your personal brand. State who you are and in what you have expertise , then the three services you will deliver.

Your experience and credibility in whatever you state upfront must be substantiated throughout the rest of your profile, including mention in your work history, your summary, your awards, your skills/endorsements and your recommendations. The max count for your Headline is 120 characters. Coming up with a headline may sound elementary; but it is not. Your headline also must reflect your top 2-3 personal branded keywords , which I will cover in the next chapter.

Further, it must resonate with your target audience and accurately reflect your skills and experience. As an example, I will share my current profile headline:

> **Jasmine Sandler (Online Branding & Marketing Consultant) www.JasmineSandler.com**
>
> Online Branding Consultant | CEO, Agent-cy Online Marketing | LinkedIn Marketing Coach
>
> Greater New York City Area | Marketing and Advertising
>
> Current: Agent-cy Online Marketing, Inc, Online Brand Comicam, Online Marketing Publication - ClickZ

My headline is within the black box. Notice that the items in my Headline are exactly the areas of expertise for which I wish to be known and hired. I am addressing all of my audience demands:

- Those looking for an Online Marketing Agency
- Those looking for an Online Branding Consultant
- Those looking to hire a LinkedIn Marketing Coach

As well, I am presenting my company brand within my headline (Agent-cy). After you review Personal Branding and keyword development in the Marketing Chapter, come back to this and start to create new headlines for your LinkedIn Profile.

3. Your Summary

Your Summary tells your story, drives your credibility, substantiates your headline and engages your target audience. You do not want a summary to read like a resume or to bore your profile visitors. Think of how you would introduce yourself if asked at a formal networking event or in providing a speech. There are some essentials to a great summary to ensure lead generation:

- Write your summary in a Word document and then bring into LinkedIn. This is important so that you do a spell check. Further, make your Summary in bullets, which is good for the reader and the Search engines.
- Highlight the core of your experience, especially whatever you decided will be your lead products or services for sale. Think of your elevator pitch and how you want to quickly get across what about you as a personal brand provides benefits to the potential buyer.
- You have 2,000 characters to summarize your achievements. Your target audience will want to see quantified results, that they then can explore more through project and work details in your profile.
- Provide your personal and company web site urls in the summary so that users can quickly learn more about you.
- Remember to include your personal branded keywords (top 2-3 keyword phrases) in your summary bullets when appropriate – again, you can see how to create your personal keywords in the Marketing chapter, under Visible profile (provide link)
- Summarize your awards and published works
- Highlight client work

See the example on the following page of an optimized Summary that follows these rules:

Summary

- 30 Years 5-star Hospitality Services Experience:
-Establishment creation
-Organizational development
-Leadership development
-Employee experience management
-Restaurant concept design
-Facility Sales growth

- Creator of Guest Services Experience Program:
http://www.fivestarcustomerexperiencedesign.com/
Method for creating brand originality and establishing long-term brand loyalty with facility guests and clients. We deliver rev- par & occupancy rate enhancement.

- Extensive background in the improvement of hospitality performance including: financial budgeting development, customer and client experience development, concept development and brand development.

- Career track record of major contributions to the growth, profitability, turnaround and overall success of several noteworthy 5-star hotels, including: Le Meridien, Pan Pacific, Key Club , Town Point , Greenbrier Country Club

- Heavy Executive Management Food and Beverage experience, including: executive level club, restaurant and food service management, banquet and catering services, and the full range of associated administrative and P&L control responsibilities.

- Creator and manager (current) of ground-breaking new concept restaurant (Fire and Vine), which has achieved the highest honors attainable for design, employee development, customer service, culinary cuisine and wine within the first two year of opening.

- Proven expertise in wines and relevant promotions

- Over two decades of fine dining experience as Executive Chef
- Professionally trained in the Culinary Arts

Awards include:
- Hampton Roads Best Restaurant Design Award, 2008
- The Prestigious Santé Award for Excellence in Hospitality and Wine Service, Fire & Vine (#1 in Southeast, #10 in Nation), 2008
- International Interior Design Association, Honorable Mention for Interior Design Excellence, 2007

4. Your Job History

As a sales professional, marketing director or business owner you probably have your resume or CV in solid form, with consistency throughout your job history. That is just the start of an effective LinkedIn profile job flow. In creating or editing your work history, you want first to write titles for each position that support your personal branding keywords. The LinkedIn Search algorithm weighs heavily on job titles. Read how to create your personal brand keyword plan in the <u>Personal Branding</u> section of this book.

Within each job description, you should go beyond the tradition resume. Remember, this is the web and your B2B target audience wants quickly to get engaged by your achievements and relevant experience. Further, they want to read recommendations of that work. This is why LinkedIn has become the tool of choice for Recruiters.

If you are selling or handling marketing for a particular company or organization, you will want to use your job history to share client case studies. Remember that your personal profile can give you the edge against competitive salespeople. You want to demonstrate how you have been an invaluable solutions partner to your clients in solving their problems while, at the same time, helping their businesses sell more, save more or gain market share. An excellent way to prove this is via Recommendations, which I will cover in the Recommendations section of this book.

Think about how the job title and description may support any and all recommendations and endorsements of your skills. So, when creating the job descriptions, you want to think endorsements and with the job title, recommendations. Let me give you a client example of the person who's Summary I referenced on last page.

Brett has recently started a new business, but brings 30 years of related experience into it. This is a trend I have seen time and again since 2010 in doing both LinkedIn Coaching and B2B Web Marketing work for start-ups. So, for those of you who have recently either started a new business or are aiding in a new project outside of your corporate work, listen in...

The name of his new company, he decided, is 5 Star Customer Experience. He provides customer experience design to hoteliers, restaurants and country clubs. What this means is that he consults with hotel and restaurant managers to provide them with a methodology for providing 5-star guest service experiences in their facilities. So, what we did was to use his incredible history in related fields (executive chef, front desk manager, back-end support manager and so forth) to build up a consistent thread and support his new position. In that his service is new, we took the opportunity to introduce it personally within the job description. We also did the same to offer a free consult and contact information. Finally, as you can see below, we titled the job in such a way to build a brand. I have also highlighted related keywords and skills and finally addressed his primary target audience, hotel managers

Work Experience

Guest Services Leader | Customer Experience Design Specialist

Five-star customer experience design

May 2012 – Present (6 months) Norfolk, Virginia Area

I am the founder and president of Five Star Customer Experience Design, a hotel guest customer design service company. I bring over 30 years of hotel and hospitality customer engagement experience to the development of this service.

Five Star Customer Experience Design has a proven business process behind it which, when launched for your hotel or hotelier group , will ensure that you build the necessary emotional connection to your guests to establish long-term brand loyalty.

We provide a free customer experience analysis to any interested hotel/hospitality corporate management groups, hotel management team, hotel general managers , guest services manager, hospitality executives, hospitality HR professionals, customer service or guest service director, sales manager or hotel owner.

Please visit our website for more information at http://www.fivestarcustomerexperiencedesign.com/.

Contact me today for your free 5-star customer experience analysis at brett@brettpatten.com

At Five Star Customer Experience Design, we excel in the following areas:

Marketing| Guest Services Experience| In-room experience|
Recommend Brett's work at Five-star customer experience design

When listing your jobs or work experience, think of all sales, entrepreneurial and marketing positions you have held and how you can craft them to engage your current target, which may differ from those in the past. Perhaps you are in a freelance or independent rep position. In that case, you want to list project based sales or marketing work. In all cases, you need a title and description that sells and drives visibility around your keywords.

A good way of understanding your personal branded keywords is to look at your LinkedIn analytics and see what people are searching for when they find your profile.

Top Search Keywords

1. jasmine — 14%
2. online — 12%
3. online marketing — 8%
4. marketing — 6%
5. pr — 2%

	Keyword	Visits ↓	Pages / Visit	Avg. Visit Duration	% New Visits
1	(not provided)	23	4.13	00:06:10	69.57%
2	jasminesandler	17	1.24	00:00:06	5.88%
3	jasmine sandler	4	1.75	00:00:17	100.00%
4	http://jasminesandler.com/ai1ec_event/learn-seo-workshop-2/?instance_id=61	1	1.00	00:00:00	0.00%
5	branding online	1	1.00	00:00:00	100.00%
6	corporate training on linkedin	1	1.00	00:00:00	100.00%
7	creating brand expert	1	1.00	00:00:00	100.00%
8	digital marketing consultant nyc	1	1.00	00:00:00	100.00%
9	how to reply to a linkedin invite	1	1.00	00:00:00	100.00%
10	jasmine marketing consultancy	1	1.00	00:00:00	100.00%
11	seo resources	1	1.00	00:00:00	100.00%
12	webmarketing slides	1	3.00	00:03:28	100.00%
13	what tools facilitate personal branding	1	1.00	00:00:00	100.00%
14	whitepaper personal branding	1	3.00	00:00:19	100.00%

Another way, if you have a branded blog or website, review your Google Analytics Source page for how people search for you.

As I have noticed, people have been searching by personal branded name, Jasmine Sandler, to find me on both LinkedIn and on my site, jasminesandler.com. This makes sense because I am a speaker and have recently started to push frequency around my workshops and consult work outside of my agency work (Agent-cy).

Also, as I always do, when you receive an e-mail or connect request from someone, ask directly for what they were searching when they found you. You may be surprised. Just today, a Wall Street executive contacted me searching Google for: How to Build a LinkedIn Page" and found my LinkedIn profile. The more you ask, the more you review your analytics, the better chance you will have to be able to target your Profile with keywords, both long-tail, as this example or direct, so that your audience can find you and engage with you.

Your LinkedIn Company Page
Chapter 4

Your company page on LinkedIn is becoming more important than ever as LinkedIn recently added opportunities for your business to promote products & services, job opportunities and company news. If you are willing to spend a little in media dollars, as well, you can create an engaging, highly targeted ad on LinkedIn about your business to specific titles, companies and in specific locations. There are multiple reasons to invest time and daily effort into your company page.

For a small business owner, once a LinkedIn user and decision maker has reviewed your profile, he or she will undoubtedly take a look at your company page on LinkedIn to see your employees' profiles as well. As a business owner, you are responsible for making sure that all company employees, currently who are on LinkedIn, are following your company. The more followers your company has on LinkedIn, the more interest your company and you will receive from the LinkedIn community, which opens up the doors for business development and PR opportunities.

For an employee of a corporation, it is important to follow your company page so that you are visible. Further, you should connect with co-workers under your company page. This will help support the company framework on LinkedIn.

Like other social media, it is important to have a LinkedIn company strategy and an appointed person to manage your company LinkedIn page. Take a look at the new company page design and opportunities here:

Branding & Sales:::The LinkedIn Way

32

A complete company page should include:
- Your company logo
- Your company overview
- Your company product and services detailed
- Your company headquarters address and phone #
- Your company website url
- Any open jobs

Similar to your personal LinkedIn profile, keeping active and providing daily news and valuable information related to your company followers is crucial. To drive up your company following, you will want to cover interesting topics to potential readers of your company page. Topics can include:

- Tips and advice related to using your products and services
- Links and comments to valuable articles, videos and podcasts
- Links to any articles you have had published
- Information on new hires
- Information on company expansion
- Information on any new company services and products
- Promotions on services and products

The Company Page in LinkedIn is rapidly looking to replace the value of a powerful industry/company database such as Hoovers.com, that which carries a hefty fee. This is why it is crucial that those responsible for a company's online brand visibility have rules in place for managing their company profile. Keeping current information on employees, titles, salary and consistent job information is important so that when others search for your corporate profile against your competition, the searcher has relevant information to make a real comparison.

Using LinkedIn Tools
Chapter 5

LinkedIn Groups

Starting or participating in LinkedIn Groups should be analogous to how you engage in professional membership associations or off-line networking groups. Your valuable contributions to and participation in Groups that align with your personal brand can net your best leads on LinkedIn. Further, by Joining client-industry Groups (if accepted), you will be able to gain valuable market data that may positively affect your service offerings.

You can locate the Groups Directory under Groups on the Top Menu Bar and going down to Groups Directory. Start by searching under your industry, target, and interest or association keyword.

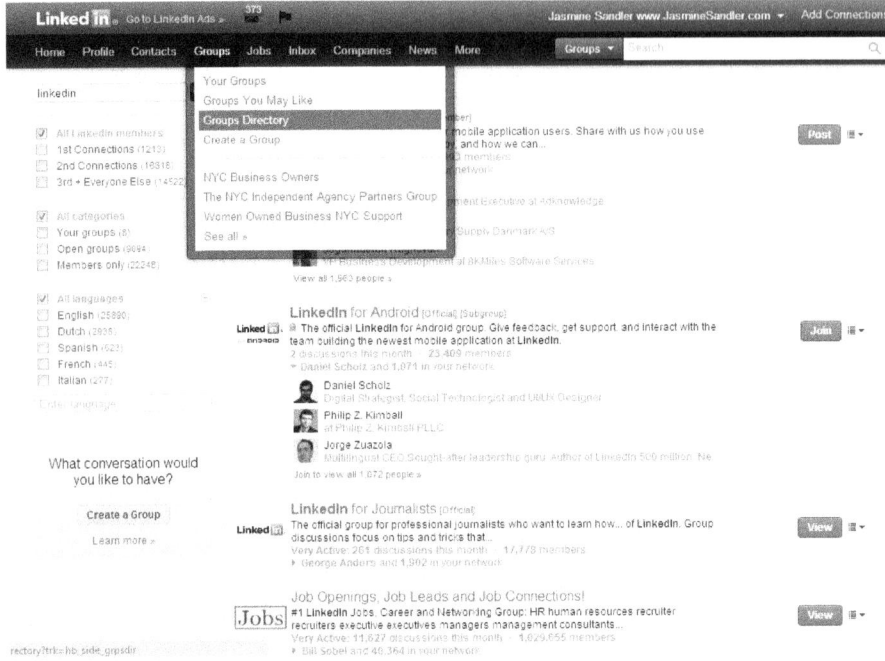

The types of Groups you should initially request to join can be any and all of the following (you can Join up to 50 Groups):

- Industry Groups (Includes Sub-industries)
- Shared Interests Groups (Community/Volunteer/Hobby)
- Member Organizations (Of which you are already involved)
- Local Business Groups (Where you do business)
- Target Audience Groups (Where you have working experience)

Once accepted, introduce yourself to the Group organizer and to the Group itself. From there, your participation in these Groups can be powerful if you share relevant content and share it consistently. Groups represent the best way to gain warm introductions, especially if the Group is based on a common interest, professional or member organization. You can send a message directly to any Group member once accepted. Simple go into Members and review those who may be local or share other common groups. Sending a personalized message that is "non-salesy" is a great way to connect with quality people on LinkedIn.

Other ways you can use Groups to your LinkedIn Sales and Marketing advantage is to like and comment on Discussions daily where you can add value or enjoy. Your fellow members will appreciate your interest in their efforts to communicate within the Group.

Within your Groups, as you would with say a local business networking group, you will want to stay abreast of member contributions and Group news. One way to do this is to see first which Discussions are popular and who is leading or contributing to these. Once you have identified qualified business professionals within the Group, you can use the "Follow" feature of that Group member to stay aware of their activity. Simply click on their photo to see all of their activity.

As an example, in one of my many business groups related to both my interests and profession (Forbes – I am an avid reader and Entrepreneurs – I serve many entrepreneurs), I found a gentleman who provides a service that could be an asset to my clients. I found him because of his high activity of quality posts in the Group. And so, I followed him, reviewed his other activity and reached out to him. It turns out, also, that he is directly connected to others in LinkedIn with whom I have an association, creating a warm introduction.

For more focused discussions within Groups, you can find and participate in "SubGroups" as available in that Group. Subgroups provide Group members with a space to discuss specific topics that may not be of interest to all Group members. As an example, I joined the Fire Safety Association Members Group because I had an alliance with one of their SubGroups: Architects, Builders and Building Officials. As a qualified target audience Group (my agency serves the industry of Construction and related fields, i.e. Architects, developers), upon my request review, I sent a note to the Group Organizer clarifying my reason for requesting an Invite. Upon your searches for Groups in the Group Directory, you will want to always read Group rules. Many Groups will not allow non-professionals in their industry to join, and you need to respect the rules.

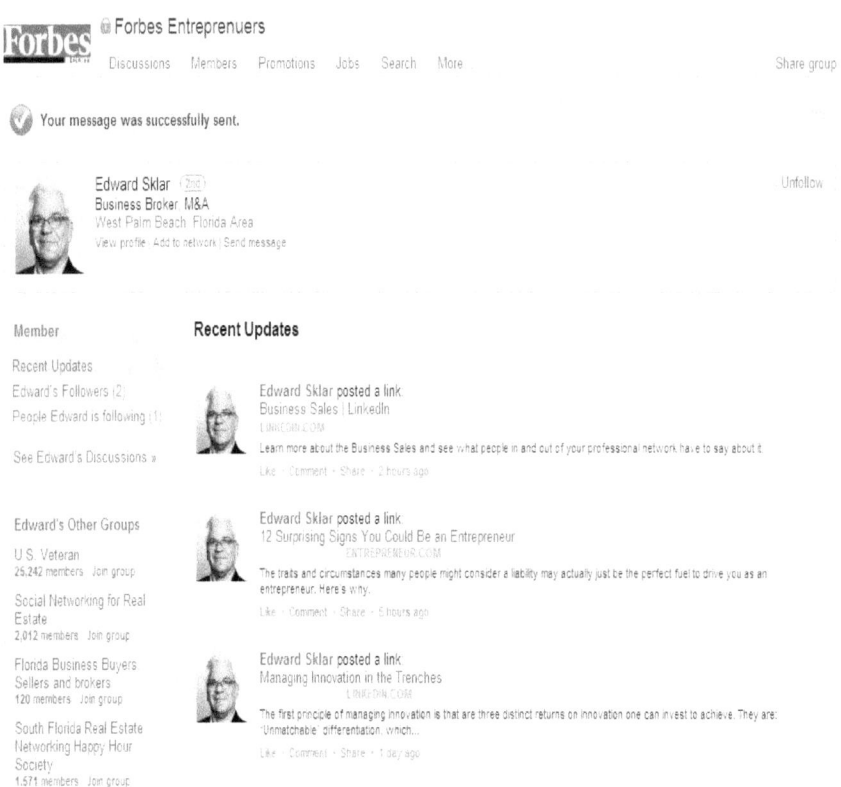

You also have the ability to suggest a Subgroup to a Group Owner by suggesting it through the Discussions tab. The suggestion will then be sent to the owner for approval. For example, you may be involved with a global group related to your industry that does not have a local subset. It would be nice for you to be able to connect with local members. You might then suggest a local Subgroup to the Group Owner.

The reason for joining Groups doesn't necessarily need to be networking. As in my case and in many cases of my clients, we use Group participation to learn from others. As I get into Personal Branding via LinkedIn Marketing later in the book, once you decide what kind of thought-leader and industry it is to which you will commit that brand, you need to be up to date with anything related. And so, for example, in that my agency provides Online Branding services to say, Architects, it is wise of me to listen and learn to professionals inside the industry within my SubGroup as above.

Other great things that you can do within Groups are the following:

- Search through the Members and find ones who are local to you or have shared interests and ask them to connect and meet offline
- Share the Group with others in your 1st Network who you feel would be good contributors or would benefit well from membership
- Post promotions for your service or product offerings in the Promotions tab of your Groups
- Post a job opportunity that is relative to the Group Industry
- Find jobs (for job-seekers) listed in the Job tab of your Group
- Find promotions of fellow members. You never know where you will find cross-promotional opportunities.

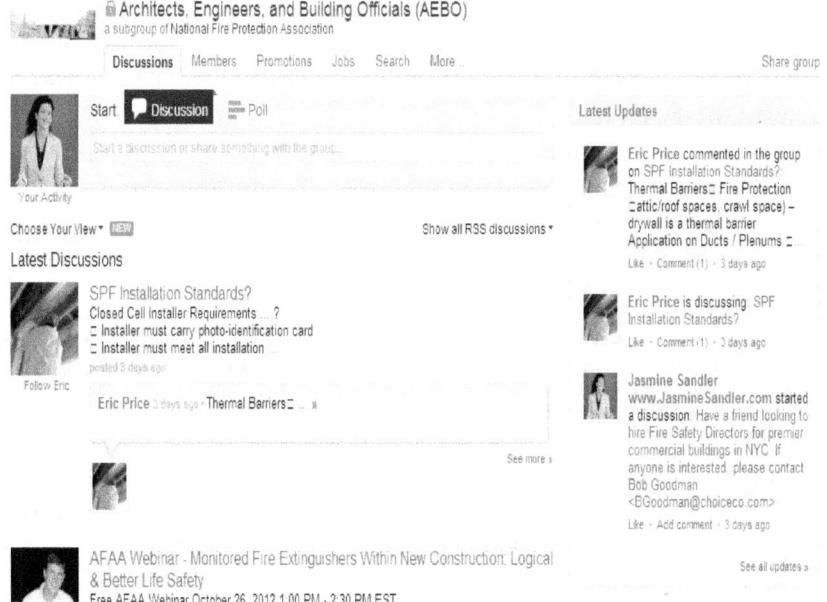

You also always have the ability to Create and Manage your own Group if you do not find exactly what you are seeking in the Groups Directory. People start Groups for a number of reasons:

- They are already running a Group as MeetUp or Yahoo Group and want to grow it through LinkedIn, and at the same time, offer it to LinkedIn connects.
- They have a passion for something that they volunteer in and want to utilize LinkedIn to develop awareness of it.
- They run or manage an existing member organization off-line and want to enable access to content for LinkedIn members.
- They run or manage a business networking group off-line and want to enable conversation related to that group to LinkedIn members

If you fall into any of these categories, please note that just by creating a Group does not mean it will be wildly successful. There are thousands of Groups on LinkedIn, all competing for the attention of its 175 mm members. You will want to go through all of your 1st connects and see where you have some commonalities. For example, in my network, I saw a heavy concentration of NYC women entrepreneurs and women business owners. I already had a mission to provide peer support to the same and thus started a LinkedIn group, called Women Business Owners (NYC).

Managing a Group means that first you need to assess a real demand for it by getting out there and asking others with similar interests if they are interested in joining (and participating). Next, no Group is successful without ongoing support and content. You will need to have a Group communications plan and commit to managing it.

The steps to creating and getting a Group going are the following:
1. Go into the Groups Directory and look to the right for +Create A Group
2. Once you click there you will need to complete the information about your Group. And so, for best practices you will need already to have thought through and to create a Group logo, a Group mission, Group rules and a Group member benefit description
3. Creating your rules: In the very least, you want to provide rules these rules:
- Members need to post Promotions and Jobs in their respective folders and not Discussions

- Define what criteria they may need to meet to be in your specific group

4. Invite people into your Group

Of course, you will want to start with your own 1st connects that make sense to the Group. You can choose to Share The Group and invite others directly from your LinkedIn network. You will want to make your invite short, yet personalized. You can also Share the Group with your other social networks such as Twitter and Facebook. You will again, want to customize your message to your different fans and followers, and keep it real.

5. Lead Discussions

They key to any Groups' success is for member activity within the Group. As the Group Owner, it will be your responsibility to lead engaging Discussions, suggest Subgroups to your Members and coordinate any offline activity. You need to think about how you can give your Group Members what they need. A good way to do that is to use the Polls feature in Groups to ask members what they may want from the Group. You can also connect directly with individual members if with a small Group to start to suggest ideas and request feedback.

6. Encourage member activity.

Like, comment and promote your member's discussions and links, if of course these are approved for the Group. If local, another way to encourage activity is to promote and invite members to local business events where you will be present. This is a great way to really connect, both on and off of LinkedIn.

Questions & Answers

LinkedIn's Questions & Answers tool can be used both for market research as well as a way for you to demonstrate thought-leadership. You can find this tool, by hovering over the More main navigation button and clicking on "Answers.". There are questions and answers in multiple categories. You can, as I and many of my connects do, use Questions as a market research tool for writing a book, developing a new business concept, to define materials in the process of manufacturing a new product, to find better/cheaper resources for your business, to ensure the validity of your service in the marketplace and more.

The Answers counterpart is a crucial activity for anyone looking to show their "expertise" in a certain business area. Once you have your personal brand defined, as I will discuss shortly, and solidify your market leader position, you then need to commit to answering questions related to your chosen category. For example, one of the categories in which I have over 10 years of experience is B2B sales. And so, under Marketing and Sales in Answers, I spend time each day reviewing questions in the Sales category to see which ones I can answer where I can provide actionable information and real value.

As a rule of thumb, unless your job is answering questions on LinkedIn, commit to 2-3 categories (max) in which to demonstrate your leadership. Answers can be ranked by the LinkedIn users that ask the Questions. If you are chosen for Best Answers, this is shown on your homepage of your profile. This is helpful in providing credibility to potential clients who review your profile.

Best Answer	**Peter Watson** I probably don't use Linked-in enough. And that's probably why I'm working only about 40% of the time as a freelance copywriter and brander, even though I work for some gigantic brands and a lot of interesting small businesses. So I could use a little advice on why you derive such benefits from these apps and services.
Best Answer	**Federico Bucchi** Could be good having, in addition to the personal page, also like a blog page where the people can write articles. For example adding the Tumblr service.
Best Answer	**Charles Caro** I don't know why LinkedIn would want to remove any of the LinkedIn Apps because each of the apps has an audience, and LinkedIn should allow members to continue using features they have grown to expect with the website.
Best Answer	**Christine Hueber** Blog and SlideShare are great for sharing your expertise.
Best Answer	**Mr. Marketology	Jeff Beale** Jasmine Thanks for asking this question. I would love to get your feedback as well once you gather some answers from the community being you are an expert in Linkedin marketing. For me the blog, slideshare, box and google presentation serve the most useful. Now every app has its own audience and purpose. Say you are a graphic or web designer. I would heavily suggest using the projects and teamspace and the creative

LinkedIn Apps

Today, there are multiple Apps available for you to use and place either on your LinkedIn homepage, LinkedIn profile or both. These Apps are meant to be used to make your Profile and LinkedIn presence more appealing to the person who visits your profile. With the new LinkedIn profile, there are rumors from those that supply the Apps(Wordpress, Google) etc. that this platform may go away with the new LinkedIn Profile. Since that is not confirmed as I write this book, I will cover the apps.

Please note that you can find all Apps under **More** on the top right of your top Navigation Bar and by pulling down to **All Applications**. Further, you can choose any App to show up on either both of your

LinkedIn Homepage and Profile or just one. The Apps you choose to be shown on your Profile should be the ones that clearly demonstrate your thought-leadership in your chosen area of expertise. For example, on my Profile, you will notice that Slideshare is my lead App. This is the only App on LinkedIn today , where I can show recorded webinars, presentations and video. Since I do most of my training and consulting using these materials, this App makes the most sense for me.

Let's look at all the current available Apps (these are changing with the new profile and I have done a LinkedIn study to see what people prefer in advance of this book):

Lawyer Ratings – For those of you that are lawyers, this is an app add in to reveal your Martindale-Hubbell client ratings, powered by Martindale-Hubbell. This can be used for individual lawyers as well as those managing legal teams.

WP – The Word Press App allows you to bring in Blog Posts into your LinkedIn profile from your wordpress hosted Blog or website. You can show Blog posts you have posted by mention of LinkedIn only. Sharing your Blog posts to your LinkedIn connects is a great way to drive users back to your blog or, as is optimal your site. I have had multiple issues with these posts not loading correctly or currently within LinkedIn and am actively troubleshooting with Wordpress. LinkedIn, at this time, does not provide direct support with inApp issues. That may change, however, upon the site investments going on at this time.

Slideshare – The Slideshare App allows you to pull in content from your Slideshare account. With a basic Slideshare account (at slideshare.net), you can pull in PPT and PDF documents to display on your LinkedIn Profile. With a Pro Slideshare account, as I have, you can pull in recorded Webinars and Videos(although Videos are not working today). As of this moment, there are some bugs with this and I have confirmed with the Tier 2 tech team at Slideshare that this is being fixed (as of October 20, 2012):

"Hello Jasmine,
I do apologize for the inconvenience. We are in the process of launching a new version of the SlideShare-LinkedIn app, with better user interface and enhanced features. It is due to be released soon, and all the existing bugs including the one you have mentioned will be taken care of in the new release. Your patience is much appreciated."

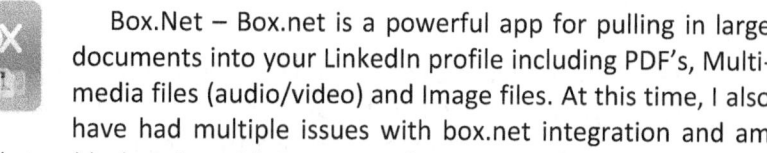

Box.Net – Box.net is a powerful app for pulling in large documents into your LinkedIn profile including PDF's, Multi-media files (audio/video) and Image files. At this time, I also have had multiple issues with box.net integration and am actively troubleshooting with Box.net tech support.

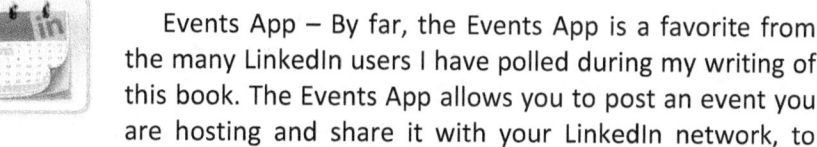

Events App – By far, the Events App is a favorite from the many LinkedIn users I have polled during my writing of this book. The Events App allows you to post an event you are hosting and share it with your LinkedIn network, to follow events you may be interested in attending and to confirm your attendance with those you are attending. Besides providing the ability for you to promote a self-hosted local event or online event, you can also utilize this to introduce yourself to fellow attendees of related events. Thus, becoming an excellent warm introduction tool.

Behance (Creative Portfolio) – A portfolio and project application, primarily used by artists, graphic designers,etc. You can show people the progress of your project. It also allows you to directly Pin it into Pinterest and share your Portfolio in LinkedIn. I have heard from many LinkedIn creative professionals that this tool has truly helped them build out their portfolio and share more with interested buyers.

Manymoon (Project Management)– An advanced project management tool that is cost effective for companies that need to manage multiple projects across several contributors. The Manymoon LinkedIn App tool allows you to share projects on which you are working with other project team members. It will also show your connects on which projects you are currently working , which may be of interest to prospective clients to see that you have active work related to their industry.

Blog Link (Typepad) – Similar to Wordpress, you can pull in your latest Blog posts but from any Blog source, including Blogger. At this time, I am also troubleshooting bugs with this App.

Reading List By Amazon- By displaying on your LinkedIn Homepage or Profile, you can share the business books you are reading with those in your network. This is a good way to engage other users who may also be reading the books you love. Sharing is what social networking is all about, so share what books have helped you spiritually or financially. If you are an author, you will want to share books you have written or contributed to so people will read and share. This helps to confirm your area of expertise.

Google Presentation – No longer working as of this date

Polls – A highly used application that has its own landing page. You can create a poll, review and vote/comment on others' Polls, as well as share Polls with your other social network pages. Polling, if done effectively, can be used for market research on a topic, product development or service enhancement. I have seen Polls on LinkedIn from everything on voting for the Presidency (which, at the time of this book, will have been confirmed) to selling techniques to ways to develop and invest. Using Polls is a great way to find out what is trending today in business and gain real-time opinions from other

business professionals on topics which may affect how you do business. I highly recommend that you peruse Polls for yourself.

My Travel (TripIt) – This App allows you to organize your travel in a mobile-friendly format. Further, it allows you to share your business travel plans with those in your network. This is useful when setting up business meetings with other business professionals in cities and countries you visit. You can share your travel within TripIt to other TripIt users and, as well, invite those in your e-mail contacts to join TripIt. TripIt opens the doors to global expansion.

FT/E-Bookshelf – This App is very useful and interesting at the same time. I am surprised, when I polled my LinkedIn network of close to 2,000 connects, that no one really commented on its use. FT provides you with recommendations of short e-book reads that are intended to provide business inspiration, education and support. The e-books come in a variety of business categories including Marketing, Sales, Leadership, Management and more. You can like and share these e-books with individuals in your LinkedIn network. By reading and sharing useful insight, you add value to your purpose on LinkedIn. I am in the process of catching up on my FT reading as we speak and highly recommend this App.

Real Estate Pro – For the many real estate professionals that there are on LinkedIn, this App is an absolute must. It provides you with real-time information on available listings in your area. With Real Estate Pro you can feature property listings and promote client transactions on your LinkedIn profile, easily share your work and completed deals with your business connections, track your market, create a following, promote your expertise and develop new business.

News and Signals

With the LinkedIn News Tool, you can follow and read featured LinkedIn Business experts news and articles. You can like and comment on articles of interest to you. LinkedIn suggests top news stories from leading business publications so that you can stay up to date and well educated on the companies and topics you follow.

With the LinkedIn Original Content Section, you can follow news by industry and by publication or news source. Engaging in this section can truly help you to stay aware of changes in your industry as well as happenings in your target industries.

With LinkedIn Signals you can monitor and edit the status updates and news from people within your LinkedIn network and within your LinkedIn Groups. This is an excellent way to stay informed of what is important to those you serve and those who you would like to serve. I highly recommend that you play with this.

LinkedIn News overall is becoming more important to the LinkedIn user experience. As LinkedIn engages journalists and reporters, therefore serving the News all under its hood, it itself becomes a real source of news information. In that, there lay many opportunities to engage the media and to reach the millions of LinkedIn news readers.

SECTION II
LinkedIn Marketing

To use LinkedIn as an effective Marketing tool, you must first understand how to create a compelling Personal Brand.

Your LinkedIn Personal Brand
Chapter 6

Your first step toward total target engagement on LinkedIn, as an individual business professional, is for you to define and commit to your personal brand. Remember that people do business with people based on their likability and trust of that person. Your LinkedIn personal profile sets the tone for how your personal brand appears and the content that you then deliver under that brand drives target user engagement.

To start to define your LinkedIn personal brand, you need to do a real assessment. Your personal brand assessment starts with determining your character strengths and how they relate to your specific area of business. To do so, ask at least 5-10 clients and or colleagues to list your strengths as they see them in how you add value as a business person.

Some examples of personal brand strengths are: Hard-working trainer, Persistent Business Relations Expert, Problem-Solving Engineer, Expert knowledge in "X", Design excellence and so on. Once you have gathered this information, you will want to choose the top 2-3 statements you feel truly describe you and ones that you can commit to serving. Remember that this commitment and direction will determine your LinkedIn content creation and delivery down the road, so choose wisely.

Prior to creating content, such as status updates, comments, articles, whitepapers, presentations, webinars and online videos for distribution via LinkedIn, you will need to determine and choose your style of communications. This style needs to relate back to and support your personal brand. Commit to a style that is authentic and one that you have seen works best for you. In other words, think about whether your humor has helped you sell in the past or if it the more serious, analytical side that draws in your target. If you are more comfortable as a writer than a speaker and can't imagine yourself running a live workshop, then you should not commit to videos or webinars. On the other hand if you shine as a presenter and crave to deliver through public speaking, then a commitment to a series of online videos, let's say, for LinkedIn distribution makes sense.

Now that you have committed to your strengths and your style, you will need to develop a content plan and related content on a daily basis. In the chapter on Creating Engaging LinkedIn Content later in the book, I will share specific content types that have delivered on impact and audience engagement, leading to qualified lead generation. The point here for you is that you need to start on your content plan early and make sure that it supports your personal brand.

Your content plan should start with determining goals upon content impact, such as reaching a new qualified LinkedIn connect, sharing content with influencers, reaching and engaging media, getting noticed by a target employer and many others. Each goal then needs to be attributed to specific content forms, such that, for example, a presentation you create has a goal of content share to potential influencers outside of your network. Once goals and content types have been determined and matched, you will want to score those matches. For example, if you commit to 5 content types with 10 goals that can associate with these types, once you deliver and measure, if content type 1 scores higher in goals value, that content type's score are rated, also higher. Content type creation and development should be viewed as an ongoing LinkedIn marketing effort.

A way to truly help you make impact with your personal brand and associated content is to know your target audience. It is crucial that you define your LinkedIn target audience at the outset of creating your personal brand. Because LinkedIn advertising and its advanced search allows you to target users by title, region, language and industry, this is how you need to think about your target audience. Let me give an example.

One of my firm's (Agent-cy) primary audiences are online and tech startup business owners. We have specific, affordable programs available in Social Media and Search Marketing for startups. Our tech startup clients have primarily come from New York City and Los Angeles. We know that this audience can be bilingual and are generally seeking to raise capital when in need of our services.

With this data in mind, it is easy for us, for example, to run a targeted ad campaign to online and software start-up owners involved in tech and VC groups in LinkedIn, the tech hot areas of Manhattan and Greater Los Angeles. We could also create valuable whitepapers and reports or deliver related client case studies to this target in related Groups. We could also take an authoritative position and seek to answer questions under Starting Up as a sub-category under Small Business Questions on LinkedIn Q&A.

Think about your target audience - where they do business, how they consume content, what information they are seeking, what their titles are, and what associations or groups they participate in. To reach and engage your audience on LinkedIn you must deliver value at all points of possible contact with them, from your personal profile to your company profile to any content you deliver and update to your daily participation in Groups and Answers.

Whether you are looking to develop a leadership position or networking for qualified new business, you need to commit to what you are selling. So in developing a leadership position, you will want to highlight your areas of expertise through stories of how you have led and inspired your employees, colleagues, clients and customers. In networking for new business, not just your products and services, but for the related packages and promotions therein, you will need to share benefits and value to your target in such a way that you build a likable story and you become their ambassador. In any case, you want to think of yourself as the best client service representative for your own brand.

To get started, write down your list of services or if selling yourself, so to speak, your specific skills and expertise.

As a part of assessing your target, you should also set your own personal brand value. What I mean by this is for you to think about how much you are worth and what type of content delivery can possibly support that price. So for someone seeking a job position through LinkedIn, for example, with 20 years industry experience, their profile of work history and recommendations should clearly illustrate their expertise. Further, that person should definitely be actively answering questions that show their expertise within industry in Q&A. That person should also be actively engaged in industry LinkedIn Groups to lead discussions on subject matter areas of expertise. At the point, then, when that person is engaged by a possible employer, he/she would have built up such credibility to support a high price for hiring them.

Think about your personal brand as a product. Where do you, as an item, fall on the price-value scale we all know so well from Economics 101. How can you become a high-demand/high-value item? The only way is for you to truly build value around your personal brand. Create your personal brand with a quality and consistency that is generally associated with market leaders such as Apple or BMW. Decide on where you will set your price, according to your market position. Are you intending on selling affordable services, but to a high volume of customers, such as affordable packages to small business owners or the converse, high ticket price items to a selected group. You need to identify and commit to your brand price and your company brand price. If you represent a company or own a company, remember that whatever value you place on yourself as a personal brand must be consistent with the overall company mission and message.

Content Creation for an Engaging Personal Brand
Chapter 7

Your Personal Brand and Company Pages need to deliver ongoing, fresh and interesting content to reach and engage your LinkedIn target audience. Again, once you define your Personal Brand and Company market position, only then can you start to execute any content plan.

The types of content that drive activity on LinkedIn can include:

- News-sharing and opinions (LinkedIn Provides a Toolbar under Tools for you to add interesting news stories and your comments to your LinkedIn status update:

- http://www.linkedin.com/static?key=browser_bookmarklet)
- Links to whitepapers
- Links to webinars and webcasts
- Links to articles you have written and published
- Blog Posts
- Polls – either that you have created or ones that you share
- Links to important press releases
- Job descriptions that you own or you find valuable to your audience
- Webinars and Presentations via Slideshare App (Video coming soon)

- Comments
- Links to Pinterest images
- Links to Blog Posts on your Blog
- Your portfolio of Creative work (via Behance App)
- Project status information (via Manymoon App)
- Discussions in Groups
- Questions in Q&A
- Answers in Q&A

To create an engaging and reasonable content plan, there are two essentials that you need to do. First, you need to determine what content is necessary for you to create and the frequency, not only of ongoing creation of fresh content; but also the of distribution. It would be wise of you to have your own editorial calendar each month defining times of week for any content that you will share within LinkedIn.

As an illustration, I am providing a real example of mine here:

Week	Blog Post	Audio Blog	Video Blog	Articles	LinkedIn Group, Answers, Post	
2012						Topic Ideas
10/14 - 10/20	x	5-10 Minute LinkedIn (tip,		x	x	LinkedIn Sales
10/21 - 10/27	x	5-10 Minute LinkedIn (tip,	x		x	LinkedIn Marketing
10/28 - 11/3	x x	5-10 Minute LinkedIn (tip,		x	x	LinkedIn Tools
11/4 - 11/10	x	5-10 Minute LinkedIn (tip,	x		x	Personal Branding
11/11 - 11/17	x	5-10 Minute LinkedIn (tip, recap, updates)		x	x	Social Media Planning
11/18 - 11/24	x x	5-10 Minute LinkedIn (tip,			x	SMO
11/25 - 12/1	x	recap, updates)		x	x	SEO Tips

As you can see, I give myself a weekly calendar of to-do's related to my content creation and delivery. All of the content creation and delivery I do is for the purposes of educating my target audience. Therefore, I am required to come up with valuable blog posts, audio files, videos, articles and status posts. Every week, I try to center my content around one topic area, for example Personal Branding, which on its own carries a load of information. My goal is continually to provide insightful and actionable content to my targets so that they are educated and continually engaged with my brand (Online Branding). I use LinkedIn as my primary B2B marketing tool; and so use it as my delivery point and sharing point for all related content.

To make something like this work for you, you must assess your resources in time to manage and money to create content, as well as any content sharing tools, such as Socialoomph.com or Hootsuite.com, both of which can help you automate your content sharing process.

Obviously your content types need to be created and delivered based on the interest and demand of your audience. Further, that it all supports your personal brand. The key is here to impress to you the fact that you will need to invest in ongoing, fresh, professional and engaging content. To help you further, let me provide you with some relative client example:

New Business Owner

Launching a Consulting service, heavy financial services, and account management background. Has connections within the industry, but now needs to reach a new target, leverage his experience and drive brand awareness around the new service.

Content Solution:

1. Created new positioning statement which leverages experience and bridges it as credibility for start of a new enterprise. Created statement as LinkedIn headline , LinkedIn project using Manymoon App. LinkedIn part of summary and within his LinkedIn Skills.

2. Edited profile to bridge components of old and new as to drive consistency in Skillset across timeline

3. Designed and created twitter marketing plan so that this person could have a way to drive immediate buzz and grow a new target base. Direct Message in Twitter to encourage Followers to join him on LinkedIn. Created message for which to engage new target audience on Twitter.

4. Set up Twitter account with LinkedIn so that status updates could be shared with new Twitter audience.

5. Set up Blog representing his new brand and pulled in Blog posts to his LinkedIn Profile. Developed and provided Blog strategy with editorial calendar for creating and delivering blog posts rich with image and video content at least 2-3 times a week.

6. Created a list of topics related to new brand of which he could commit to creating related content on an ongoing basis. Created an editorial calendar he could manage using Google Docs.

7. Provided our photographer and online video personnel to him to help create compelling content.

8. Put measurement and tracking system in place so that he could enable trackable links on all content.

9. Provided him with a tutorial on how to manage his blog, create short links, and assess marketing performance via analytics and funnels by goals.

10. Gave him a messaging plan for status updates, invite replies and warm introduction requests

11. Agreed to Answers Categories (2) that he would focus on building his thought leadership

12. Assessed target Groups and came up with Intro message and daily time plan for reviewing discussion threads (and commenting)

Daily Time for Content Development/Delivery

It's not enough to spend money on books and content creation; you will also need to commit to or have an employee commit to, on your behalf, managing your personal brand on LinkedIn. Please note if you do decide to have someone else manage your personal brand, you will need to make sure you are spending time guiding, managing and approving what they do on your behalf to maintain your authenticity. You will want to work with someone who has direct brand management experience, especially with LinkedIn or at least, with a social media background.

Once you have a content plan, you should follow it and measure it for its effectiveness on building brand awareness and target engagement on LinkedIn. I do not put a time limit to LinkedIn content marketing as others may do because I use LinkedIn as a source of news information and connecting in real time with my connections, so I am a heavy user. As business professionals in Sales and Marketing, you should have a daily work schedule and time for Marketing. The amount of success you have from LinkedIn is directly related to the amount of efforts you put in to developing and delivering valuable content and helping others in your network (provide valuable information, make warm introductions and so on).

So that you can have a manageable LinkedIn content marketing experience, I have highlighted for you some LinkedIn daily task essentials:

- Updating your status to provide content that is valuable to your network. This can be events, promotions, links to interesting articles and more
- Participating in qualified Groups
- Answering targeted questions that share your expertise and support your brand
- Updating your profile with fresh content (links to articles, blog posts, images, videos, audio files)
- Engaging in original content, news and signals at least 20 minutes a day (again no one rule for amount of time here but at a minimum do this) so that you might engage on that level or share valuable information to your network

Getting Found on LinkedIn
The SEO connection
Chapter 8

As part of your personal branding on LinkedIn, you will need to determine and solidify your personal keywords. These are the keyword phrases which you want to be found by your target audience when they search in the People search in LinkedIn. Success can be not only your direct target audience; but also think about how the media or influencers may find you.

If you have decided upon in your personal brand style, which we covered, that you want to be a speaker and thought-leader for your industry, then you might have keywords pertaining to public speaking of "x" industry. Of course, your main personal keywords should relate to your expertise and the products and services you sell. You need to think of and analyze your personal search keywords similar to how you do so for your corporate brand. Remember that we are talking about driving visibility to YOU as a brand. And so, now that you have gone through the exercise of determining your strengths, your services and your target audience, it is time for you to determine your personal brand keywords.

You should start with the top 15 keyword phrases for which you want people to find you. I will use myself as an example. I started with these:

1 LinkedIn Trainer
2 LinkedIn Coach
3 SEO Consultant
4 Paid Search Consultant
5 Digital Marketing Consultant
6 Social Media Consultant
7 Social Media Marketing Consultant
8 Online Marketing Consultant
9 Web Project Manager
10 Strategic Planner
11 Strategic Planning
12 Business Strategy Consultant
13 Personal Branding Consultant
14 Personal Branding Coach
15 Personal Branding Trainer

Your next step is to run a keyword idea generator in Google Adwords Keyword Tool - **Google AdWords**
https://adwords.google.com/o/**KeywordTool**

    Enter in your 15 keywords where provided and then Google will deliver you with expanding keyword phrase ideas and associated search volume as well as search market competition.

    When I entered in my 15, I received over 100 keyword ideas with associated volume and competition. So that you understand, in case you are not familiar with these metrics, what this means I will share a sample and explain. Google pulled a few of my important keywords as above "web project management" and "online marketing" and suggested the following as potential keywords I may want to buy (on a Cost Per Click basis under Google Adwords) or that I want to optimize for in Natural Search. The competition % here indicates the competition present in real-time for people buying these keyword phrases in Adwords. The number of searches indicates both globally and nationwide, how many individual searches there are on the particular keyword phrase in a month. As a general rule of thumb, unless you have or are spending heavily in time and money on a specific keyword phrase related to your brand, you will want to stay away from highly competitive keyword phrases. You also don't want to invest much into those with little or no competition

Keyword	Competition	Global Monthly Searches	Local Monthly Searches (United States)
project management software	0.96	246000	90500
software project management	0.96	246000	90500
online project management	0.96	74000	27100
project management online	0.96	74000	27100
web project management	0.93	49500	22200
project management tools	0.92	60500	22200
free online advertising	0.92	49500	18100

Also, as you will see above, some of the suggested keyword phrases are what we call negative keyword phrases, such as project management software. I don't own or sell project management software or project management tools, but I do offer web project management. And, I have multiple jobs and client recommendations as a web project manager, so that keyword now is a viable personal keyword phrase for my LinkedIn Profile. But with high competition, it will take a lot of effort in SEO practices to gain top visibility in both LinkedIn People Search and Google Search. So for an example sake, I will then take "Web Project Management" back into the keyword tool and search for more relevant, yet lower competitive keywords.

Keyword	Competition	Global Monthly Searches	Local Monthly Searches (United States)
[web project management]	0.9	1300	390
[web based project management]	0.96	1900	1000
[online project management]	0.97	8100	3600
[social media management services]	0.96	720	390

Since all of my keywords are highly competitive, I choose to start with 2 keyword phrases directly related to the services I provide which have actual search activity, but at least under 1 for competitive rank.

This is just the beginning. You will need constantly to refine your keywords by doing further keyword analysis, using more sophisticated tools than the Basic Google Adwords tool. These include Wordtracker, Compete.com Search Analytics and many others. You can find an exhaustive list of keyword tools and other SEO tools on my consult site at http://jasminesandler.com/recommend-tools-to-automatefacilitate-seo-best-practices/ (As this is a book on LinkedIn and not an SEO book).

Once you have ascertained your keywords, which, again reflect and substantiate your personal brand, work history and recommendations (or endorsements), you will then need to use them effectively in your LinkedIn profile to drive search (LinkedIn and Google) visibility. Some rules to follow:

- Use your keywords in your Headline
- Use your keywords in your Job Titles
- Use your keywords in your Skills
- Use your keywords in your job description
- Create a list of skills related to each individual job description and make it a part of that job description.

Client example:
At the end of one job description, he has:
"At Five Star Customer Experience Design, we excel in the following areas:

RevPar enhancement | Occupancy rate enhancement | Hotel Management| Front Desk Service | Guest Services| Guest Services Manager| Hotel Client Service| Restaurant Management| Restaurant Marketing| Guest Services Experience| In-room experience|"

Other important points on personal keyword development for LinkedIn

- Identify your personal keyword phrases based on the services you sell and can substantiate with related experience within your LinkedIn profile

- Do your homework and analyze these keywords to identify medium competition and good search volume

- If local, focus on local keyword identifiers (geo-target)

- Make sure you use your top 1-3 keyword phrases as appropriate throughout your profile, including within your custom LinkedIn url.

Leveraging LinkedIn across all your Web Marketing
Chapter 9

As my previous client example on content marketing details, leveraging your other social media activity and activity on the web, in general, can support your LinkedIn marketing efforts and enable better results.

LinkedIn status updates allow you the ability to share with either your company or personal Twitter page. Remember that in Social Media Marketing, you need to be where your users are and that most often users are not on a singular network. Internet behaviors show that users use Social Networks for different purposes (for example: Twitter for news, LinkedIn for developing business relationships, Facebook for getting deals on consumer products and so on).

If you are looking to drive a personal brand position on the web, you will need to invest in more than just a LinkedIn profile and management thereof, although this is crucial and should be your first step. Having a well designed and developed Twitter page for your personal brand, with updates from your LinkedIn page, can engage Twitter users looking for experts to contact you at the LinkedIn level. There are many other reasons and ways you can use Twitter to drive brand awareness on the web; but this is a LinkedIn book so I will stick to the Twitter basics for this reason. For Twitter Marketing tips, feel free to visit my personal blog on www.jasminesandler.com.

Your website or blog or website with blog (preferred) should support your LinkedIn profile. If you own your website (business owner) here are some rules to follow for leveraging your site with your LinkedIn Marketing efforts:

1. Make sure you have a link to your LinkedIn Company Profile on your site
2. If you have committed to a personal/professional blog, make sure you have a link to your LinkedIn personal profile on your Blog.
3. Use the LinkedIn status update tool to share your blog content, with a link back to the individual Blog post. With the LinkedIn status update, you can choose to share with everyone, your connections only or specific Groups. And so, if you have Blog Posts that would be better suited to some Groups, you can choose to share with them only. I have found that this works well to engage specific users over specific content related to their job functions. To enable, simply choose the option to share with Groups under status and then start to type in group names. Your Groups will come up and you can make those choices.

If you are a Sales professional or Manager or Marketing Manager and representing a firm, you can still certainly leverage your company's website content for your LinkedIn marketing efforts. I run into this quite often with clients who work for the large financial services, real estate and insurance firms. They want to drive a personal brand on LinkedIn, but have to adhere to compliance issues within their Marketing departments. For them, I say you can utilize your company's marketing communications, while at the same time, creating your personal brand on LinkedIn.

As long as your messaging about the company you for which you work is in alignment with those rules, you can still voice your opinion on why your product or service is better. You should utilize the materials provided by your marketing department to drive LinkedIn connects to engaging content. Referencing your company's website case studies, news and service materials can help your company and you drive in more sales.

If you have invested in Paid Search Marketing or a formal SEO practice, you can and should utilize your reports therein to determine what keywords and ad groups (with PPC) are driving the most traffic and interest. Once you have that defined, you can then use LinkedIn Advertising and its networks to drive Leads or start to create and deliver relative content in the form of LinkedIn Discussion posts, Promotions within your Groups and status updates to engage users back to your site.

Many LinkedIn users are also heavy Facebook users. As I mentioned before, your next client could certainly be on Facebook or at least your next influencer. You want to make sure you are covered in all areas. And so, with Facebook you want to make sure that you have your LinkedIn profile URL and LinkedIn Company URL present on those pages so that your Facebook fans are familiar with your LinkedIn presence.

In general, what you push out on LinkedIn needs to be visible to other users at every point of your online marketing efforts. Your Twitter followers need to know about your latest slidedeck on Slideshare that is present on you LinkedIn profile. Blogging and Blog posts (frequent) can and should be the cornerstone for your content delivery (especially if your Blog resides on your website where you are selling your products and services). One of your Facebook calls to action should be to get your Facebook users to connect with you and follow your company on LinkedIn. Make all of these efforts support each other and then you will have brand consistency, efficient LinkedIn Marketing and easily measurable results.

Advertising On LinkedIn
Chapter 10

LinkedIn provides you with the opportunity to reach business decision makers globally in virtually every industry. LinkedIn Advertising can be very powerful if done effectively because it provides detailed targeting by location, gender, title, age group and industry. Advertising on LinkedIn can be cost-effective in testing the demand for new services, new products and paid events. The opinions on LinkedIn advertising varies, but with certainty targeted advertising for specific lead generation around lead magnets such as free whitepaper downloads, free reports, free webinar signups, trial software programs and such, has proven highly effective.

You can test Advertising on LinkedIn by going to the footer of your LinkedIn page and clicking on Advertising. From there you can set up an advertising account under your own profile or your Company Profile. Creating an ad from your Company Profile will add more to your Company page and show the ad when people are looking at your Company. In LinkedIn you can test ad variations and use imagery to lead your ads. Similar to Google advertising, you get a headline and two lines of copy, up to 28 characters.

You can collect leads directly into your LinkedIn profile for your ads and you can create a business account tied into your Company page. Collecting leads directly on LinkedIn gives the LinkedIn user the ability to act without wasting any time and is excellent for you to generate inbound leads quickly.

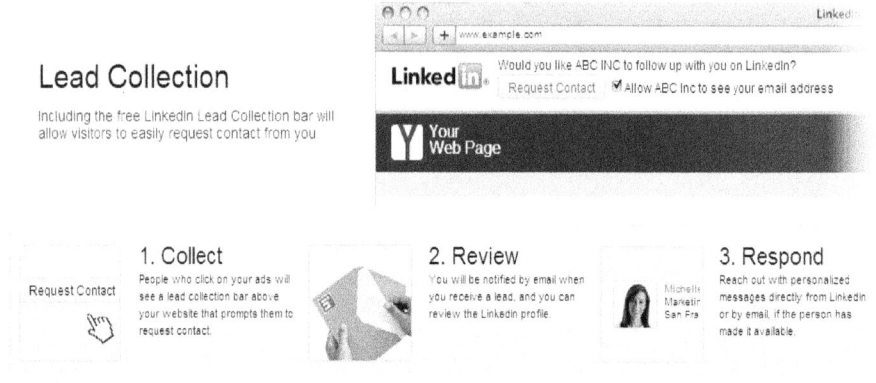

LinkedIn Advertising can be very effective for inbound lead generation. It is worth a test. Here is a quote from a recent advertiser:

"50% of our paid inbound leads come from LinkedIn. LinkedIn is our most cost-effective online marketing channel."

Matt Johnston
VP of Marketing at uTest

Your LinkedIn Marketing Plan
Chapter 11

As I am sure you know, every successful business person has a business plan with targeted goals and a measured way to reach those goals. LinkedIn Marketing is no different. You should have a targeted LinkedIn Marketing plan crafted by a LinkedIn Marketing professional or you can try it for yourself. If you decide to DIY, make sure you have these 10 essentials covered:

1. A plan for updating content daily based on the content planning and management instructions I have provided.
2. A plan for providing value to your 1st connects.
3. A plan for developing warm leads through Groups participation.
4. A plan for measuring effectiveness in Groups.
5. A plan for keeping an accurate and engaging profile.
6. A plan for Company Profile communications.
7. A plan to keep your employees on point on LinkedIn.
8. An apps plan.
9. A plan for recommendations and endorsements.
10. A plan for managing connections.

Now, let's get into the heart of what we are all looking for: QUALIFIED SALES THAT WILL HELP OUR BUSINESSES GROW and how to get there using LinkedIn.

SECTION III: SALES

Creating & Building Your LinkedIn Network
Chapter 12

The first part of selling on LinkedIn is for you to create and establish your initial 1st connects network. Initially, you will want to pull in existing databases. In LinkedIn when you go into Connections, you will find the ability to enter in your existing POP e-mail accounts, such as Gmail, Hotmail , Yahoo and AOL(God forbid☺) and have LinkedIn search for users already in the LinkedIn universe and suggest that you add them. With new users joining every 2 seconds (October 2012 stat from LinkedIn), more than likely your contact is already on LinkedIn. If they are not, you also have the option of asking them to join. Obvious, immediate first connects should be current clients, colleagues, peers, association members, alumni and business networking friends. As a general rule, whenever you ask someone to join your network, personalize the message. There is NOTHING I hate more than an impersonalized or completely salesy request to connect to me. If you take a look at my LinkedIn profile, in the Ways to Contact section, I provide a direct message to people that I appreciate a personalized note with an intro on how and why they found me and a little bit on why they want to connect.

Under LinkedIn Tools in the footer of your LinkedIn Homepage, you will find ways to import and utilize your existing CRM tools to engage those leads and accounts for more LinkedIn connections.

As an example, this is what the Outlook import looks like under Tools. You also have the ability within LinkedIn to create a personalized signature for engaging with your Outlook recipients.

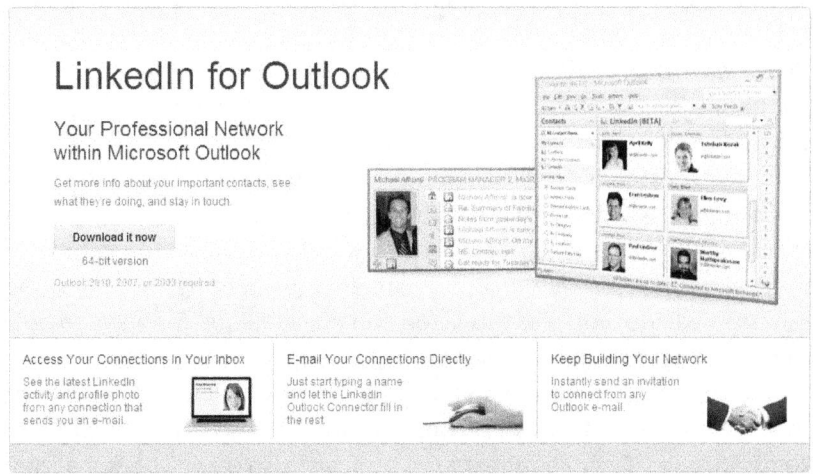

As I am sure many of you in Sales are Salesforce.com users, there is great news here. Not only can you pull in your Salesforce leads into LinkedIn via an API provided by LinkedIn, but also With "LinkedIn Integrate for Salesforce", you can pull in lead prospect profiles right into Salesforce and get insight within the CRM on each individual user. This is available with the LinkedIn paid Premium Sales accounts, Navigator and above. LinkedIn provides tech support on other CRM's as well. If you are using a CRM that is not listed in the LinkedIn toolbox, contact them directly to discuss.

Once you have established your initial network, you should constantly be thinking about growing a qualified LinkedIn network. Anytime you attend a business networking event, meeting or conference, make sure you get the business cards of those with whom you may want to do business and from there, request to connect with them on LinkedIn. Any smart Sales professional will take into account the conversation that was had and make a personalized introduction when requesting to connect. Further, than just connecting, of course, we want to create long-term business relationships on LinkedIn.

Taking the time and effort to create real relationships

Your first LinkedIn marketing goal is to drive buzz and brand awareness around your latest campaign, product or service. Your next is to then engage direct relationships with decision makers within your target audience. Remember then, that we are talking about human connections. You need to take these conversations off-line as in an actual phone call, or if local, a meeting. This simple step will fast track your way to your next sale.

When interested LinkedIn clients come to me, one of the questions they always ask is "How Can I turn my Connects into Clients?" The key is to create a real relationship. One simple way to do this is to invite your connect to a call (or meeting if local). In the meeting, as any good salesperson will do, you want to listen and engage, look for ways to be a resource and commonalities. More than likely, you will find something of which you have in common in business. This will give you a reason for further connecting with this person. Perhaps it is by joining a common LinkedIn Group. Once connected, you can also send personalized, valuable content to them and follow them on LinkedIn to support their content.

The more you assist your connects and their LinkedIn experience, the more you will see that that person will do the same for you. Just this morning, I received a call from a prospective client who was referred to me by a LinkedIn connect with whom I have created a strong relationship. This exemplifies the fact that all of your LinkedIn connects do not necessarily need to become your end clients. Further, it supports that salesy introductions are untargeted and poor LinkedIn etiquette.

LinkedIn Sales Etiquette
Chapter 13

Let's talk about LinkedIn communications etiquette for a moment as this is something that constantly comes up when I deliver corporate LinkedIn training. Because there are so many opportunities to connect with people (via Openlink , Inmail, Group Member messaging, etc.) there are also many opportunities to deliver an offensive personal brand message. No one likes an aggressive overly salesy approach from a stranger.

My first rule of LinkedIn etiquette is to get to know who someone, his company and responsibilities and personalize the message as much as possible (sometimes LinkedIn re-sends past invites that were on delay without your knowledge and for this you can only do damage control). So, as is in professional sales, you first want to define a targeted Sales plan that supports that market's demand for your product and the role/responsibility of the job function. Once you have developed your plan and your list of key people with whom you would like to do business, you should review their LinkedIn profile and Company profile. You should also take a look at their website and other web pages (Twitter, Facebook, Pinterest, etc.) to gain an understanding of what their own marketing and sales goals are. With their LinkedIn profile you may find common Groups or that they are an expert in a knowledge area (via LinkedIn Answers) that matches your industry/service. With real information, it then is much easier for you to send a targeted, personalized message.

Just this morning, I received 4 requests for invites from 4 web design companies in India, all telling me that they can design a better web site for me. Had they taken a look at all of my announcements and my company site at agent-cy.com, they would have seen, that exactly at this time, we are re-designing our website! Unbelievable! Absolutely zero etiquette. At the same time, I have also in the recent past received Inmails and Requests for Invites with personalized messages based on common Groups, which have led to business relationships and client work.

As a part of this topic, let's explore ways to connect with people and etiquette. To Inmail, Message or Request to Connect first? My philosophy on this, as I am sure you can tell, is to get to know someone first before you let him into your circles. And so, I always appreciate a message (from a fellow Group member) or Inmail first that is personalized with the following:

- Why you looked for me – if you read something I wrote or a comment I provided
- How you found me – If referred by someone, who?
- Why you want to connect. Honesty is the best policy here.

Tomorrow, for example, I have a call arranged with a gentleman from an online video production company who sent me a vague Inmail on "working together." I responded and asked him directly whether he wanted to hire me and my firm for Online Branding or was he looking for an agency partner? He replied that he was indeed looking for a partner to help him sell more. I appreciated his honest and arranged the call.

- Your contact information and links to your webpages

Another important LinkedIn etiquette topic is your etiquette in Groups. First, when you choose to join a Group, make sure you read their rules before you make the request. Most times, Groups are well moderated (unless an Open Group) for whom they accept into the group. If a moderated Group (closed), make sure you fit the criteria for the group. Once you are admitted into a Group, use the Boards wisely. Discussions mean valuable Group suggestions, links to valuable articles, announcement of events, questions on topics that the members can answer and Polls that may serve the Group. Your comments and likes within these discussions should illustrate your knowledge and real opinions of the content. The promotions tab is just that. If you are looking to sell or promote anything, use the Promotions tab first. The jobs tab is for you to post real jobs that make sense to the work experience of the members and at the same time for you to look for related jobs (if you are a job seeker). The rules are the same for Subgroups, which are niche focused topic groups within certain Groups.

The beauty of Groups is that you can make warm introductions to members within a group, in that you have a common association. Although, it may seem warm, you still do not know this person, so go back to how you will message them by first understanding their business and goals and do not assume that they will want to talk to you right away. Also, just because they share a common Group does not mean that they will want to business with you. All you can do is a make a personalized, polite request. Just as in professional (solution) sales, you must observe the fact that people are busy and simply provide them with information that you feel will serve them until such time that they are ready to do business. This points to the importance of having a LinkedIn Sales Plan.

LinkedIn Sales Planning and Scoring
Chapter 14

Having a Sales Plan that is targeted and reasonable (to your resources) is the first step in actively selling via LinkedIn. In that Plan you will need to identify several critical areas:

1. Your target audience – who are they, where are they, how do they/do not use LinkedIn for Marketing, what is important to them, what are their profiles and company pages
2. You value proposition – what makes you different. We talked about this quite a bit in the Personal Branding section earlier. You want to also take this to the company level. Take your time to review your competitors (whether individual or corporate) and how they are using LinkedIn to market
3. A plan for building lists for new lists (Lead Builder) and one for warm leads (Groups and referrals) as well as Hot leads.
4. A plan for connecting off LinkedIn with your connects including how (phone, Skype, live meeting) and frequency (5 a day) (30 min/1 hour).
5. A plan for lead follow-up and management (via a CRM)
6. A content management plan (as discussed earlier)
7. A LinkedIn advertising plan as covered earlier, as applicable.

8. A way to track success. You will need to analyze how much time and effort you are putting into these areas and then assess your client sales. You need to keep in mind your sales cycle per service and per client. What I mean by this is that you may have some transactional based products and services as well as or instead of solution based services. Solution-based services have longer sales cycles and those need to be accounted for in reviewing your success.

As a B2B sales executive and Sales Manager for years myself, I follow the same principles in LinkedIn Sales that I will now share with you:

1. Have a Sales plan that is targeted and reasonable
2. Commit to working your Sales plan daily
3. Use your CRM tool daily. Use it in combination with LinkedIn Lead Builder and Profile Organizer to find qualified leads and manage your sales process
4. Constantly provide valuable information to your leads (once you have gained an understanding of their industry and business)
5. Look within your LinkedIn network and LinkedIn Groups for ways to gain warm introductions to your leads
6. Attend LinkedIn announced events, group member association conferences, group member off-line networking events as much as possible where you have the opportunity to meet your leads
7. Take your LinkedIn conversations off-line. Follow-up is key via phone, e-mail and meetings (if agreed to by your leads)
8. Follow a proven Sales process: Introduction – education – consistent follow-up with valuable information – available when lead is ready to buy – close.
9. Follow your lead's company and profile on LinkedIn to stay up to date on what is important to them
10. Always keep your network fresh. Bring in new connects from off-line engagements and networking.
11. Segment your connections by leads, influencers, partners

Just as we do "Lead Scoring" in Sales, the same can be said for how you value your LinkedIn connects. For fun, I have created my own "LinkedIn Connect Scoring System" Feel free to use and follow:

My example:

Title	Revenue	Budget	Call to Action	Need Identified	Decision Timeline	Lead Score
Entrepreneur	1mm	3,000	referral	marketing strategy	Dec-12	
1	1	1	3	1	5	2

5 Lead	4 Lead	3 Lead	2 Lead	1 Lead
CEO, Owner	VP	Director	Director	Director
20-50mm	15-30mm	10-20mm	5-10mm	250k-1mm
100k	60k	20k	10k	5k
attended work	referral	whitepaper	whitepaper	lead form
Marketing AOF	Online PR	Online Br	SEO/PPC	Strategy Only

So that you understand my system and target scoring example per above, let me explain. My ideal target (for my agency, Agent-cy @ www.agent-cy.com) is a C-level person of a small to mid-sized company. Our target industries include:

- Commercial Real Estate (Sales, Consumer Products,
- Professional Services (Law, Insurance, Financial, Medical)
- Technology Consulting and Services

In the example above, which I took from a conversation I had today, I give this person a lead score of a 2. This person is a lawyer with a solo practice (Score 1) who was referred to me by one of my LinkedIn 1st connects (Score 4). In assessing his needs, I identified the need for help in Marketing Strategy Only (Score 1), a Budget of $3k (Score 1), annual revenues of less than $1MM (Score 1) a decision timeline of December 1 (Score 4). The total being 12/6, leaving me a lead Score of 2. In this case, I know that this is on the lower end of my lead value and so one of my immediate actions is to thank the referrer with a meal (they are local) and explain to him (after drinks) that I am growing my business and my ideal clients are larger companies, but thank you for the referral and here is a free meal. Having a lead scoring system and managing it gives you a birds eye view of what is going on in your Sales efforts.

For the sportspeople out there (especially my fellow hockey players), it is like being the defenseman and seeing how the whole field operates, instead of just one single area of vision.

As the CEO of my company, I constantly review our revenue leaders(services) average length and size of deal, how our marketing (lead sources) are or aren't working, our best clients in terms of revenue, marketing budget, industry and title and our sales cycle. And so, I have created a leads scoring system that takes into account all of these parameters so that I can measure the marketing-sales engine on a frequent basis and work to drive niche marketing/efficiency/business expansion.

So how does my lead scoring system work within the parameters of selling on LinkedIn. Easily.

In LinkedIn, I have my calls to action set up:

1. Attend one of my workshops, webinars or teleseminars.

I set up all of my events using the event app in LinkedIn. I then announce these events to my target Groups in discussions or promotions (depending if it is a free or paid event); in my status update and make my events visible on my LinkedIn homepage and profile. I also announce these events on my LinkedIn company page for Agent-cy.

2. Gain referrals.

I manage a LinkedIn Group called Agency Partners. Within this Group, I encourage other marketing and PR agency owners to work together and share client work, as appropriate.

Post a satisfied client, I ask for a LinkedIn recommendation (I have 70 or so at this point). I also ask them if they wouldn't mind being a reference. In this way, if they say yes, when my target sees my LinkedIn recommendations, they can then actually directly contact them and discuss my or my agency's work.

Most importantly, once I develop real relationships in LinkedIn, I educate them on my lead scoring system, so to speak, so that they know who to refer to me.

3. **Download a Whitepaper.**

In my Profile Summary, I provide the direct link to my free whitepaper download http://jasminesandler.com/free-white-paper-how-to-develop-an-engaging-personal-brand-in-linked/

I also provide a link to when people in my Groups ask questions around personal branding or using LinkedIn for Marketing.

Because I have set up my Whitepaper free download as Pay with a Tweet, every time someone downloads it, it is Tweeted. Then those that follow me on Twitter that aren't yet my LinkedIn connects are driven to my LinkedIn profile.

4. **Lead Form Sign Up**

As part of my networking on LinkedIn (both online and offline conversations), I follow-up with a timely e-mail to share links to my websites: (Consulting and Training – jasminesandler.com) (Strategy and Execution – agent-cy.com). On my lead form page on both sites, I give people direct instructions on why they should contact me or Agent-cy.

5. **E-Mail Newsletter Sign Up**

Many times, my LinkedIn connects come directly through LinkedIn, so what a better way to extend the relationship than to introduce them to my ongoing communications (newsletters). The newsletter sign ups live on both sites, so once I share my sites, which both have Blogs and Multi-media content to keep users engaged, a user can sign up for my newsletters.

Since my newsletters alert people of upcoming events , service enhancements and provide online marketing tips (rich content), they act to provide referrals and direct transactions.

Recommendations & Endorsements
Chapter 15

Oftentimes I hear my fellow LinkedIn connects wondering how important recommendations and now endorsements are as a way to drive credibility in advanced of Sales. As part of your Personal Branding promise, the Recommendations should support and be authentic to that brand. Further, they must be from real clients and business partners with whom you have done business. Just because someone provides you with a recommendation for your work, does not mean that you need to return the favor as LinkedIn will suggest. If you have no working experience with the person in that you were never their client nor witnessed their work, it would be unprofessional for you to provide a recommendation. All of the LinkedIn people I Polled in advance of this book agree that Recommendations are far superior as a credibility factor to Endorsements. With recommendations, as well, you can add them as testimonials to your Blog or site. Wordpress actually has a plugin for that (as well as everything else).

Endorsements were developed in LinkedIn's response and current attempt to match a Facebook experience, using things such as "Likes" and "comments" at every turn. Also, currently, as of today's date, the

LinkedIn endorsement tool has bugs, such as duplicating suggestions. Endorsements can work well for people whose work you have witnessed, but otherwise are not or have not been a client. These could be strategic partners. I, for one, have thousands of strategic partners, as a 15+ year networker, and have provided endorsements to their work, which I have witnessed or as a referrer of them to my clients.

So that you know how to recommend someone, it is as easy as going to their Profile and going to the drop-down next to message and under Engage you will find Recommend or Endorse.

Another feature, not used as often as people should, I believe, is Sharing a Profile with someone in your network. In this way, you are giving someone direct visibility into their target audience. I use this for those whom I strongly believe are the best in their fields and can help strengthen the growth of one of my clients. I also utilize Sharing for referring people to each other as intros. I do this quite a bit and found it is an excellent way to help and become a real resource to my connects.

Emphasis on Necessary LinkedIn Sales Tools in Premium Accounts
Chapter 16

As I stated earlier, there are several reasons to upgrade from a Free account to paid, but for me the most invaluable tool for any Sales professional is Lead Builder. This allows you to do targeted lead search by industry, company size, function, and geography. Further, you can save your searched lead list and then save the profiles of the people you want to build relationships with.

To take it a step further as you should, look to see who you know who knows that person. Ask politely for a warm introduction. Something I must highlight here is that LinkedIn will suggest many potential connects to the person whom you want to be introduced to. You can choose whomever you want and send them an intro request note. This does not guarantee that you will be introduced. You always want to, as a rule of thumb, follow up with the person for whom you have asked a connect. Many times that person does not really know the other and cannot make a valuable introduction. You may have to go through 10-15 warm connects until you get a direct introduction; all the while following up with all of the people whom you have asked to connect you. Remember to follow up off of LinkedIn. An e-mail or phone call can end up saving you a lot of time in waiting for a response.

Secondly, I do think that Profile Organizer has some real merit, especially for folks who are not using an outside CRM tool. In the very least, this tool allows you to save profiles and make notes so that when you go into Profile Organizer who have a track of your leads and conversations.

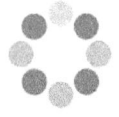

OpenLink – as a Premium member, you can Inmail free to others in the Openlink network as well as receive free messages from others in Openlink. This is a great tool for you to be able to Inmail anyone in Openlink and expand your network. Many sales professionals and business owners use Openlink and by contacting them using your target audience keywords, etc. under Lead Builder, you may indeed find an influencer who can lead you to your next client.

Deciphering LinkedIn Analytics
Chapter 17

So you put all this effort into LinkedIn to gain visibility and engage your target audience, so what about monitoring and measuring Your LinkedIn Success?

You can start by searching or having someone else with a Premium account (to see more searches) in People under your branded keywords to see where you come up.

With a Premium Account, you can see who Viewed Your Profile and go back to unlimited records. In seeing you viewed your profile, if they allowed you to see who they are (you can choose to be anonymous), you can view their Profile and see if you would like to contact them. In the View Your Profile area, you can also see # of views of your profile on a certain day. This is useful to track how well your marketing is affecting target interest. You can also view how many times your profile appears in Search. This is directly related to how well you have optimized your Profile for Search. This is why, as I have stated before, that as part of your LinkedIn Marketing Plan, you update your profile often to reflect new work. You can also view your keywords in terms of what people searched to find you in percentage break-down. This will show you if people are searching by your brand (name) as in my case (Jasmine 13%) or your keywords (Online Marketing 11%) for example.

As you analyze these stats above with Sales, it should be clear how your marketing efforts affect how people find you and who engages with you. Remember that LinkedIn Marketing is a daily practice. The more you learn what is working versus what isn't the more that you can alter how and where you spend your time.

Afterward: LinkedIn Member Services: Hopeful Changes

As a realist (a New Yorker), I can say that not everything about LinkedIn is peaches and cream. Just as I am an advocate for LinkedIn as a B2B Marketing and Sales tool for Branding and Sales, I am equally an advocate for the heavy LinkedIn users such as myself. There are major issues affecting our experience on LinkedIn and I need all of you reading this book as well as your LinkedIn connects to stand up and make some noise. This is the only way that change is made.

Since I don't believe I could say it better, I will start with a LinkedIn answer from a true LinkedIn heavy user and I dare say, tool expert:

"It is clear LinkedIn management is not doing enough (anything) to serve its membership, and this is seen in numerous ways at virtually every level within LinkedIn."

LinkedIn seems to think the website (whatever they opt to pass off as a website) is the "product" and its members are simply coming to the glorious LinkedIn website because the website is such a good "product".

In fact, it is the LinkedIn members that are the "product" not only because it is the members providing 100% of the website content but also because it is the members the Premium subscribers paying US$8000+ per seat want to find on the website.

As I recently tried to explain to another LinkedIn member, on LinkedIn the members are the "fish" in a pond, and it is the Premium subscriber that pays US$8000+ to get a "fishing" license along with the advertiser looking to catch one of the "fish" in its "net". LinkedIn's primary job is to keep the "fish" in the pond, and the only ways they can do that are to both provide good activities such as the LinkedIn Q&A Forums and LinkedIn Groups for the "fish" to swim in but also *good* customer service. At present LinkedIn is failing miserably on both counts.

Of course, LinkedIn doesn't really understand the value of keeping the "fish" happy because, at the present time, the money continues to come in because most of the "fish" haven't made it clear they want more and nobody has been clever enough to create a new pond for the "fish".

In many ways LinkedIn is like AOL, which was riding the crest of a wave with ever expanding membership and revenues until suddenly the AOL members started to learn AOL had *not* invented the Internet and the Internet was *not* AOL. There was a time when most AOL members really thought the Internet was AOL.

The "typical" LinkedIn member spends less than seventeen (17) minutes per month on LinkedIn, which is horrible.

LinkedIn members must start to take a more active part in letting both LinkedIn and abusers know they want more. When a LinkedIn member sees something that is *not* right they should do whatever they can to report the infraction. Only then will the nonsense stop and the waters of the pond will be right for all of the "fish". '

In defense of my colleague and support of pushing things forward to make our LinkedIn experience the best it can be, I have, almost on a daily basis, made my voice heard in terms of feedback on things that just don't work or changes that hurt the LinkedIn member user experience.

So let me tackle the particulars from my perspective. At this juncture, the Apps are still present as LinkedIn makes it 175MM+ rollover of profiles to the new look and feel. However, it is well rumored that Apps will go away once the rollover is universal. In my Polling of other heavy LinkedIn users, we want to tell the powers that be at LinkedIn that a lot of these Apps have real use and we want them to stay and also get fixed.

Of the 20 or so responses I received from my Poll, across the board heavy users agreed that every App has its own particular use for its own type of business professional. Of the Apps that were favored most heavily (a good cumulative 80%) were the Wordpress and Typepad Blog

Apps, Event App and Slideshare App. Even within these Apps, I have witnessed multiple problems. I have been troubleshooting these problems all the way with the limited App customer service I have been receiving:

1. Slideshare – The video show on profile, even for Pro slidehsare and premium LinkedIn members (of which I am both), does not work. I have literally gone all the way up the Slideshare chain and no resolution.
2. Wordpress PlugIn – Pulls in old posts, won't pull current. I have been pressing forward only to be told by WP tech that the App is going away
3. Typepad Plugin – Shows duplication of posts. No tech support available.
4. Event App – No instructions, rhyme or reason for how event search results appear. No support.

That is just the beginning. As my colleague had stated so precisely, for the LinkedIn users that spend both the time and considerable money (with Premium subscriptions) LinkedIn customer service is TRULY lacking. We would like this to change. Adding a "Share Your Feedback" sidebar does nothing if it is not resolved. I have "shared my feedback all too well" with no responses. As is customary with websites that are there to earn money, there is no number to call. And I quote:

"We want to help you in any way we can. ...We don't currently offer phone support."

This reminds of back in the day when I was consulting for a small website selling gun parts. I told the CEO, if you guys just have a phone number to call and some good customer service people answering the phones 9-5EST, your business will take off. Today and only 7 years later, that CEO is a multi-millionaire and running several web businesses with GREAT customer service.

And that is my point, customer service in a highly competitive environment (social networking sites) can be the difference between a market leader and loser. I already know, in my own technology circles here in NYC , of entrepreneurs and existing service companies looking to replicate and enhance the LinkedIn model. As a LinkedIn heavy user since 2005, I don't want to see that happen. I would rather work alongside the team who manages and posts daily about all the LinkedIn great changes on the LinkedIn Blog, to help them shape the best user experience for its members.

And so, I ask all of you reading this book to report any bugs, problems in customer service and abuse practices in the Share The Feedback tool. Share this request with your LinkedIn connections, and of course, this book.

Thank you

Thank you for reading my book.
Here's to your Branding & Sales Success: The LinkedIn Way.

Author's Bio

Jasmine Sandler is a B2B Social Media veteran. She has worked with hundreds of corporate clients to help them use the web effectively to drive up brand awareness and ultimately sales. Miss Sandler heads a team of B2B Online Marketing professionals under her own full-service web marketing and PR agency, Agent-cy Online Marketing, Inc. established in New York City in 2006. At the core of Agent-cy Online Marketing is Online Branding for both companies and executives. As a LinkedIn Marketing pioneer, Miss Sandler has been actively using LinkedIn as a B2B relationship vehicle since 2003. Jasmine is a corporate LinkedIn Marketing trainer and coach to business professionals around the world. With a background in technology, marketing and corporate sales for such organizations as IBM, Citigroup and AT&T, Miss Sandler has a deep understanding of how to engage business customers online. Miss Sandler provides digital marketing consulting on corporate projects and is an Internet Marketing industry speaker, presenter and writer.

Miss Sandler can be contacted through her consulting web site at http://www.jasminesandler.com. On the site, she also provides frequent online videos, presentations, webinar recordings, podcasts and articles on how to achieve success in both online branding as well as social media customer engagement. Her agency, Agent-cy, has a website at http://www.agent-cy.com, which provides ongoing client case studies and success stories on effective web marketing practices.

Branding & Sales
The LinkedIn Way

Jasmine Sandier

www.ingramcontent.com/pod-product-compliance
Lightning Source LLC
Chambersburg PA
CBHW061515180526
45171CB00001B/184